ENDORSEMENTS

"Ken Ulmer is one of America's new voices, rising with a penetrating call to pragmatic spiritual dynamics. As a Christian leader, he stands tall; as a servant to society, he stands out; as a friend, he stands trustworthy; as a man of God, he stands close—in touch with our Father, that he might be in touch with Him whose touch can change the world."

—Jack W. Hayford
Chancellor/Pastor, The King's Seminary
The Church on the Way
Van Nuys, California

"My dear friend, Bishop Kenneth Ulmer, is one of the most outstanding, creative preachers of our time. With *In His Image*, he has given us a creative biblical treasure that will not only capture our minds, but will also move our hearts toward a God whose heart is moved toward us. Reading this book will compel you to love God more deeply and to worship Him more fully!"

—Dr. Crawford W. Loritts, Jr.
Speaker, Author, Radio Host
Associate Director, Campus Crusade for Christ

"In *In His Image*, Bishop Kenneth Ulmer reveals from Scripture just how completely and fantastically our great God and Savior loves and cares for us, illuminating facets of His being that many believers have no doubt never considered."

—Dr. Bill Bright
Founder of Campus Crusade for Christ

IN His

IMAGE

IN *His* IMAGE

AN INTIMATE REFLECTION OF GOD

DR. KENNETH ULMER

WHITAKER
HOUSE

Editorial note: Even at the cost of violating grammatical rules, we have chosen not to capitalize the name satan and related names.

IN HIS IMAGE: An Intimate Reflection of God
(Revised and Updated Edition of *The Anatomy of God* by Kenneth C. Ulmer)

Kenneth C. Ulmer
333 West Florence Ave.
Inglewood, CA 90301

ISBN-13: 978-0-88368-993-6
ISBN-10: 0-88368-993-6
Printed in the United States of America
© 2001, 2005 by Kenneth C. Ulmer

1030 Hunt Valley Circle
New Kensington, PA 15068
www.whitakerhouse.com

Library of Congress Cataloging-in-Publication Data

Ulmer, Kenneth C.
    In His image : an intimate reflection of God / Kenneth C. Ulmer.
        p.   cm.
    Summary: "Inspires a deeper relationship with God by exploring how to be more like Him based on the references to God's anatomy in the Bible"—Provided by publisher.
    ISBN-13: 978-0-88368-993-6 (hardcover : alk. paper)
    ISBN-10: 0-88368-993-6 (hardcover : alk. paper)
    1. God—Attributes. 2. Image of God. 3. Anthropomorphism. I. Title.
        BT130.U57 2005
    231'.4—dc22   2005025513

1 2 3 4 5 6 7 8 9 10 11 12 13 **ɰ** 14 13 12 11 10 09 08 07 06 05

CONTENTS

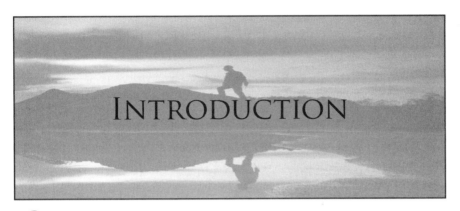

INTRODUCTION

No one enters this world and lives in uninterrupted perfection and happiness. After all, we all encounter unexpected potholes along the road of life—sometimes caused by our own bad choices. But every tragedy, trial, or wrong turn results in an opportunity for God to return us to His path for us and becomes an opportunity for us to allow God to remake us in His image.

But if God is a Spirit, as it says in John 4:24, then what exactly is His image? This book answers that question while revealing the physical attributes He wants us to reflect.

There is an old story about a gifted sculptor who one day instructed his assistant to bring into his studio a mass of mud-covered, jagged marble. The assistant struggled to drag the huge rock into the studio and finally, with sweat dripping from his brow, he proclaimed to the talented artisan, "Master, this rock is a mess! What will you make of such an unattractive pile of dirty, unpolished stone?" The brilliant sculptor stepped back and gazed intently at the unwieldy mass in front of him. His eyes swept slowly over the dusty marble, and after a few moments he announced, "I see...a picture in my mind!

IN *His* IMAGE

I see...a beautiful stallion! Yes, that's it. A magnificent stallion with blazing eyes, a flowing mane, and flared nostrils!" With a shrug, the assistant responded, "But how will you get such a masterpiece out of this ugly, craggy rock?" The visionary artist smiled and answered, "I will take my hammer and I will take my chisel and I will chip away and chip away—everything that does not look like a horse. And when I finish, the only thing left will be my masterpiece: a magnificent stallion!"

That is precisely what God wants to do with each of us: take our crinkled, bent life and shape and coax and love us into a magnificent work—His masterpiece.

It does not matter how much dust or dirt, rocks or ridges, cracks or crevices you've accumulated. God wants to chip away at everything in your life that does not look like Him. He wants you as His self-portrait.

God Himself is the divine image and Jesus Christ is the model, the very image of God on earth. Trust Him, follow Him, obey Him, and your life will become His personal masterpiece, in order that you become a river of inspiration, a light of encouragement, and a path of enrichment to all who come into your life.

May you always live *In His Image*.

—*Dr. Kenneth C. Ulmer*

ONE

ANATOMICALLY SPEAKING

"Father, I want to know Thee, but my coward heart
fears to give up its toys. I cannot part with them
without inward bleeding, and I do not try to hide
from Thee the terror of the parting. I come trembling,
but I do come. Please root from my heart all those
things which I have cherished so long and which have
become a very part of my living self, so that Thou
mayest enter and dwell there without a rival. Then
shalt Thou make the place of Thy feet glorious.
Then shall my heart have no need of the sun to shine
in it, for Thyself will be the light of it,
and there shall be no night there."
—A. W. Tozer, *The Pursuit of God*

The scene is not an uncommon one: midnight ticked
by long ago, and everyone in my house is asleep
but me. I am cocooned in my office, wondering if
tomorrow's—now *today's*—sermon will miraculously appear
before me. It never does. But I confess, I really don't mind.
For it is in these still hours that I allow my one true obsession
to take flight: pouring over Scripture, dissecting research

material, and sifting through the myriad windows in the latest Bible study software...to the end that I might catch a new glimpse of *Him!*

> *I beseech thee, show me thy glory.* (Exodus 33:18)

Moses was more than merely curious when he asked for the Lord's visible presence on Mount Sinai. Although I don't presume to claim that mighty prophet's "friendship" with God, I have at times been powerless to control the begging of my own soul to see more of the One who cannot be contained by heaven and earth. I am the psalmist's hart, panting for just a sip, a tiny taste, of something I cannot live without. It has been the most fruitful pursuit of my life! I have never been disappointed. All of my attempts to fathom our unfathomable Father have been rewarded with equal amounts of harvest and hunger. I continuously seek Him, even as I luxuriate in what I've already found.

> EVERY ACT OF GOD IS ROOTED IN THE DEEPEST DESIRE OF HIS HEART—TO BE KNOWN BY US.

I realized something long ago: God enjoys this pursuit as much as I do. He's not being coy. He doesn't play "hard to get." He *wants* to be chased...and He wants to be caught. That's why He eggs me on. Ours is a game in which we both win every time I get another look at Him. Second Corinthians 3:18 says that the more we see Him, the more we mirror who He is. That is why each glimpse we get of Him adds more glory to His name.

Every act, every thought, every motive of God is rooted in the deepest desire of His heart: that He be *known*. From

Genesis to Revelation, His Word is a divine detailing of who He is. Every man, woman, parable, and proverb in the Bible adds another line, shade, color, or contour to the magnificent canvas of His story. The signs and wonders He performs in the Holy Scriptures, as well as the ones He is still performing every day in our lives, are not mere stunts executed to impress us. He doesn't need our approval. His mighty miracles were not done so that men would believe, but rather that men would know Him in *whom* they believe. Every prophet, priest, apostle, and teacher in the Bible had but one assignment: to proclaim God's personhood. Today, every evangelist, pastor, minister, and Christian has that same mandate.

> *All things were made by him; and without him was not any*
> *thing made that was made.* (John 1:3)

God made *everything*. He is also *in* everything, which means that all of God's creation and handiwork helps us to see our Father, the Creator. In this book, we are going to take a look at the different ways in which physical man reflects the image of God, who is a Spirit (John 4:24). We will endeavor to understand the person and nature of God by looking at what He says about Himself in physiological terms. We are going to do this by using a theological and literary device called "anthropomorphism," which is simply a ten-cent word you can cut in half to make two five-cent words that make sense: *anthrop* (or *anthros*), meaning "of, or pertaining to, man"; and *morphism*, which means "form" or "shape." Therefore, seeing God in anthropomorphic terms simply means that we will see (and better understand) Him in the form of man, or in human terms.

God's most obvious effort at self-revelation can be found in our own mirrors. Yet, while He is omnipresent, omnipotent, omniscient, and holy (and those are just the punctuations on His calling card), God is not literal flesh and blood—He does not have a body. He is, as Jesus told the woman at the well, a *Spirit.* Nowhere in the Bible is there a reference to "the body of God." The closest representation is the body of Christ the Messiah, God incarnate, God in the flesh. Yet, while the Bible does not speak of God having a body, there are numerous references to specific body parts. That doesn't mean He is a collection of disjointed ghostly limbs and organs floating around in the cosmos. It means that He has chosen to reveal Himself to us in concepts and ideas that we can understand in the physical realm. He has chosen to make Himself known to us "earthly bodies" by relating our physical anatomy to His Spirit.

In this book, we will explore how our own anatomy is God's most complete biography of Himself. It's as though He uses our bodies to play a kind of spiritual *hide-and-seek* with us. In the midst of a world filled with visible, audible, tangible, and mental options between good and evil, the clearest look we can get of God is literally right under our noses. Our Father created us in such a fashion that we, even in the finite limitations of our humanity, are capable of both visualizing and comprehending our infinite and limitless God. In other words, we were physically designed so that God could teach us about Himself.

AN INVITATION TO INTIMACY

Over the years, I have received thousands of invitations to banquets, weddings, fund-raisers, awards dinners, and various other events. In deciding whether or not to go, I look at the information relevant to my schedule and commitments. If I attend, I know where to be and what time to show up. I don't think about it much further than that.

My wife, on the other hand, can often tell just by looking at the invitation what kind of gathering it will be. She can tell from the paper stock, the ink, the wording on the card, and the quality of the lettering on the envelope if we can expect succulent filets and delicate confections, or rubbery chicken and boxed cake. I count on her to tell me if I'm dressed appropriately. If we're expected to make a donation, she has the checkbook. Seldom is she taken by surprise at these gatherings.

I, however, feel that some invitations should come with disclaimers, so I won't be caught off guard. Something like, *Event will actually be more tedious and less significant than it appears on this invitation.* Or, *We advise eating a good meal before coming to this luncheon if bad food is not to your liking.* What I'd really like to see, though, is this: *We plan to start on time, but our plans usually don't work out at these affairs.* A lot more could be known about an event and the people putting it on if more attention were paid to the invitation.

> OUR OWN ANATOMY IS GOD'S MOST COMPLETE BIOGRAPHY OF HIMSELF.

The Bible is actually a divinely written invitation to eternal fellowship with the Almighty. God drafted it personally through some 40 human authors, in 66 volumes, 1,189 chapters, 31,173 verses, and 774,746 words. No expense was spared on this invitation. Jesus gave His life to deliver it to you. Moses, Isaiah, David, John, Paul, Jeremiah, Daniel, and many others became living pens through which the Holy Spirit extended the Father's request for the pleasure of your company.

God's pursuit of us is a deliberate and methodical act of grace. He did not save us to take us to heaven to keep Him company. He is not lonely. We're not doing Him a favor when we worship Him. His chest doesn't stick out any farther because we thank Him. He'd still be awesome if we didn't praise Him. He would exist in all His glory if we didn't believe in Him.

If you don't understand the complete lack of God's need for you, then you might miss the wonder of your salvation. If you think His motive for saving you is selfish in any way, then you might miss that He is utterly in love with you. And if you see His love for you as anything less than perfect, you know Him as less than perfect (which means you really don't know Him); and above all, He wants you to know Him.

> I CAN'T EVEN CONSIDER FOR TOO LONG WHO GOD IS WITHOUT BEING REMINDED OF WHO I'M NOT.

Knowing God...I am often overwhelmed at the task of wrapping my mind around just what that means. He is I AM, the One in whom and by whom all things exist. He is holy. Every aspect of His being is infused by, and enveloped in, His holiness. His righteousness is a holy righteousness. His power is a perfectly holy power. He's more perfect than "perfect" could ever be. As pure as "pure" is, it is far less pure than God. He is justice and truth. He is merciful, all-knowing, ever present, and unchanging from everlasting to everlasting.

Before I know it, my ponderings and ruminations on God's wonderful attributes lead me onto personal ground that vexes me. Paul called it his "wretchedness." David put it this way:

What is man, that thou art mindful of him?   (Psalm 8:4)

I remember the man I used to be. I know the man I still am. It seems almost cruel to me that God would give me a mind to understand how unworthy I am to receive any understanding of Him—much less *from* Him. It is puzzling to the point of painful frustration to look at all that I have and to know what it cost Him to give it to me. I don't know if I could do the same for Him. I cannot even imagine sacrificing my only son for Him (and He knows that). My love for Him is not as great as His for me. That's why He is God and I am not. I can't even consider for too long who God is without being reminded of who I'm *not*. Like David, I wonder why He bothers with me. At that point, my intellect fails me—and it is at *that* point that God is at His most magnificent!

In His Word we find:

His **eyes, which roam throughout the Earth** and see us no matter where we are. (2 Chronicles 16:9)

His **powerful arms**, capable of snatching us from the jaws of every devouring enemy. (Deuteronomy 33:27)

His **loving smile,** which makes all grace abound toward us. (Numbers 6:25)

His **fingers**, which knitted us in the womb. (Psalm 8:3)

His **strong hands**, daily guiding and directing us through dangers seen and unseen. (Psalm 139:10)

His **attentive ears, which** hear our cries. (2 Samuel 22:7)

His **nostrils**, with which He inhales the fragrance of our prayers and exhales blasts at those who persecute us. (Psalm 18:8, 15; Exodus 15:8)

His **loving heart**, which desires to be close to us, and aches when we wander too far from Him. (Psalm 33:11; Isaiah 40:11)

HIS PHYSICAL CLOSENESS

God's motive for making Himself known to us bodily, physically, is to invite us to reflect on Him intimately, to see Him as truly approachable, reachable, and touchable. He desires intimate, close *relationship* with us, His beloved creation.

It is accurate to say that God's ways and thoughts are far above ours. His breadth extends far beyond the capacity of the universe to contain it. He knows everything about everything. He is singularly powerful, awesome, and glorious. Only He could have established His throne. No one appointed Him to His position, and no one is "God enough" to wrench it from Him. But if we limit our view of God to those things that make Him heightless, groundless, bottomless, and boundless, then we have placed Him where He least wants to be: *beyond our grasp!*

> *Am I a God at hand, saith the* LORD, *and not a God afar off? Can any hide himself in secret places that I shall not see him? saith the* LORD. *Do not I fill heaven and earth? saith the* LORD. (Jeremiah 23:23–24)

If man was created to show God at His most caring and intimate, and we were made in His image (and "God is love", according to 1 John 4:8), then we are bodily portraits of God's love. Knowing how wretched we are, that concept can create quite a clash within us. That is why, to see Him anthropomorphically is to see Him in terms of His love for us, and not vice versa. In this context, even our unworthiness bears witness, because

18

God's mercy and grace overcomes how undeserving we are of His infinite love. However, infinitude without intimacy is the unkindest portrait we can paint of God. It would be like a child grabbing at an object that is being continually kept just out of reach. The longer the game goes on, the more frustrated the child will get. Eventually, he will give up. And we will too, if we limit our understanding of God to the aspects of His nature that seem to keep Him "away" from us.

As we examine the physical image of God in Scripture and see how men, women, and entire nations had their lives influenced and shaped by their understanding of it, a cycle begins to emerge: as God gradually discloses Himself to us, He progressively creates within us an increased capacity to comprehend each new disclosure. He stretches our imaginations just enough to hold a little bit more of Him. Then, once we are comfortable with that revelation, He stretches our imagination a little bit more, and we draw even closer.

> GOD'S MOTIVE FOR MAKING HIMSELF KNOWN TO US PHYSICALLY IS TO INVITE US TO REFLECT ON HIM INTIMATELY.

This progressive disclosure of God cannot take place without our consent or our active involvement. The more we earnestly seek and desire that He reveal Himself to us, the quicker the goal is realized: *to bring us closer to God.* At every stage, we are required to respond to God by making a choice that will signal our desire to continue on with Him. And, as with all divine "co-laboring" efforts, our participation is subject to (and limited by) the presence of *sin* in our lives.

THE SIN FACTOR

Sin separates us from God. Separation from Him prevents us from seeing Him, communicating with Him, coming to Him, and being changed by Him. Sin, if allowed to build up in our lives, will bog down the workings of every spiritual pursuit. Prayer is hindered by sin. Gifts become powerless in sin. Wisdom becomes carnal and ineffective when sin is present. Character is destroyed by sin. Honorable efforts are thwarted by sin. Vision is obscured, ministry becomes fruitless, and the path to God is obliterated by the darkness of sin.

Every believer should be in the habit of allowing the Holy Spirit to do a periodic sin check. Like David, we should cry out:

> *Search me, O God, and know my heart: try me, and know my thoughts: and see if there be any wicked way in me.*
> (Psalm 139:23–24)

David was a man after God's heart not because he was the picture of sinless perfection, but because he was always willing to see sin as God saw it, and always willing to respond to it the way God responded. He exposed himself to the light of God's statutes, and if he found himself lacking, he moved immediately to confess and repent. David's life was marked by his relentless pursuit of God.

> *One thing have I desired of the LORD, that will I seek after; that I may dwell in the house of the LORD all the days of my life, to behold the beauty of the LORD, and to inquire in his temple.*
> (Psalm 27:4)

Everything David ever wanted was wrapped up in his longing to be in the holy presence of God. So, too, should all of our aspirations be shaped and colored by a desire to see God—and an unwillingness to accommodate the presence of sin.

When we submit ourselves to God's way, His will becomes clear to us. His desire to be known by us becomes obvious, and the cycle of working that desire out is put into operation.

REVELATION

Revelation exposes a part of God's physicality to our view, uncovering something previously hidden from us. God can't bare Himself to us all at once. We couldn't handle it. The consuming fire of His holiness would destroy our humanity. So God mercifully unveils Himself to us a bit at a time according to three criteria: our desire to see, our ability to see, and our need to see.

God never forces Himself on us. Love is always a choice. He chose us; and He is willing to risk not being chosen by us, in order to allow us to experience the divine nature of His love in its fullness. Thus, God does not reveal Himself to the son or daughter who doesn't want to see Him. Throughout Scripture, we are told to seek God, set our affections on Him, run after Him, grope for Him, call out to Him, and lean toward Him. All of those activities require effort on our part and are always preceded by a preference or tendency toward God.

Once God knows that we desire to see Him, He then considers our qualifications for receiving His revelation. While sin disqualifies us as recipients of the things of God, we are also disqualified by our refusal to act on the most recent revelation He gave us. God is not wasteful; He doesn't move us on to a new lesson until the old one is learned. He won't give new revelation where the current one withers in our fear or unbelief. If we refuse to receive from Him, we diminish our ability to receive more of Him.

All revelation is given from God on a need-to-know basis. If you need to know that God hears your cries, then He will reveal His listening ears to you at just the right time. If you need to know that His hand will provide for you in the wilderness, He will reveal it. If you need to see God's eyes, He will not show you His mouth. You may think that what you need to see in your crisis is provision from the hand of God. But what God may want to show you is the peace that comes from the awareness that His ears hear your cries. It is God who addresses your need, but it is also God who determines what your need is. Every revelation will be according to His purpose, and that purpose was established even before your need was.

Hebrews 11:6 says that before we come to Him, we must first *"believe that He is."* Therefore, our response to the revelation of God is simply to see what He shows us, and to accept in that moment something that has been uncovered and placed before our spirits for our perusal.

RECOGNITION

Once our spirit has beheld a particular aspect of God, our mind must then make the proper recognition (or attribution) concerning it. This recognition places the revelation in a spiritual archive of understanding. Where revelation says, "I see something," recognition acknowledges, "I see *God.*" It is at this point that every believer must accept or reject responsibility for what he now knows.

I've been to board meetings where men and women raised their hands and cleared their throats in an attempt to make it obvious to the person conducting the meeting that they wanted to be seen and heard. But until the chairman "recognized" them, they couldn't speak.

God makes it obvious that He wants to be recognized. Recognizing Him involves a twofold act of directing our attention to Him and then communicating our willingness to hear Him. Like anything else with God, recognition is for our benefit, not God's. He's no more important because we recognize Him. Rather, recognition of Him is our acknowledgment that He is more important *to us*.

Have you ever seen somebody coming toward you in the distance, and you decided to walk on the other side of the street because you didn't want to deal with them at that moment? The fact that you never had to engage in conversation with them doesn't negate the fact that you did see them. Some people try to play that game with God. They see Him, but they think that if they don't acknowledge Him, they will be absolved of the responsibility to respond to Him. Let me tell you a little secret: God saw you coming before you saw Him! There is no path wide enough for you to avoid Him.

> GOD NEVER FORCES HIMSELF ON US; HE IS WILLING TO RISK NOT BEING CHOSEN BY US.

The same spirit that allows us to recognize God also shows us when something or someone is not of God. Not every dollar offered to help you out of a jam comes from the coffers of God. Recognition is affected and sometimes distorted by the condition of our hearts. A heart fueled by fear, bitterness, anger, lack of forgiveness, or pride will weaken a person's ability to recognize whether or not something is from God. If we're not using our spiritual eyes, the enemy's hand can look like the hand of God. For example, a woman who harbors a fear of being alone may recognize an unsanctified, unsanctioned love affair as "God-ordained."

Recognition must always be run through the filter of the Word of God. In order to recognize God in someone or in the midst of a situation, we must be able to place it next to what God has already said in His Word. If it doesn't line up, then we have to consider that what we are experiencing is not a divine revelation.

Our response upon recognition is to then *move*. Move toward whatever is acknowledged to be of God and away from what is not. In Revelation 3:20, Jesus said, *"Behold, I stand at the door and knock: if any man hear my voice, and open the door..."* Notice that the door doesn't open until the person inside hears a voice. In fact, Jesus implied that the opening of the door is preceded by the person's understanding and acknowledging that Christ is definitely the One knocking at the door. He said, *"If any man hear **My** voice."*

Whenever God reveals Himself to us, He always allows us the opportunity to accept or to ignore Him. By ignoring Him, we ask Him to stop talking, stop moving, and stop acting on our behalf. And He will back off until we say otherwise. But our acceptance—our *recognition*—of God, invites Him to add color, dimension, and depth to our relationship with Him.

RELATIONSHIP

> *And I say unto you, ask, and it shall be given you; seek, and ye shall find; knock, and it shall be opened unto you. For every one that asketh receiveth; and he that seeketh findeth; and to him that knocketh it shall be opened.* (Luke 11:9–10)

Most of us have read the above verses of Scripture in our studies, heard them preached from a pulpit, or caught them during spiritual conversation. They comprise one of the more obvious illustrations of reciprocity that we enjoy being in relationship with God. We ask, and it is given. We seek, and then we find. We knock, and the door is opened unto us.

It is plain that we are not by ourselves, adequate within ourselves, or able to acquire what we need all by ourselves. There are some things we need that we don't have, so we ask God for them. There are other things we have that are not sufficient, so we seek them out and God leads us. There are some areas of sufficiency that God wants to add to, so we inquire at the doors He places in front of us.

> WHENEVER GOD REVEALS HIMSELF TO US, HE ALLOWS US THE CHOICE TO IGNORE HIM.

As we consider God's desire to show Himself to us, what makes the passage in Luke 11 special to us becomes clear when we consider the grammatical tenses of the verbs *ask*, *seek*, and *knock*. The tenses indicate continuous or repeated action. In other words, Jesus is telling us to keep on asking, keep on seeking, keep on knocking, over and over. The implication is that we will keep on receiving, finding, and having doors opened to us in response. This is how we experience ongoing relationship with God.

When the Lord reveals a part of Himself to us and we recognize His presence in our lives, it should lead every willing heart to examine every implication of that revelation. For example, when I see the protective arm of God shielding me from harm and danger, and I acknowledge Him in my life as my strength and buckler, then I begin to understand how He kept me when I didn't know how to call on Him. I start to get a little braver about my tomorrows because I know that He will be watching over me. I see His mercy, grace, long-suffering, and love colored with His desire to protect me. As I study every facet and fold of this newly understood aspect of God, my prayers take on new depth and boldness. My praise is expanded, and my worship is more complete. The more relationship I experience with God, the more I want with Him, so the more I ask, seek, and knock.

Relationship is the blossoming of the curiosity created by every new unveiling of God's person to us. It is through relationship that intimacy knits us to the very heart of the Almighty. As God teaches us more about Himself and reveals more of His heart to us, we fall more in love with Him and we get an increasingly clearer understanding of how in love with us He already is.

As our intimacy with God increases, an intriguing paradox occurs within us: God appears to be more loving, while we appear to be less lovable. As He becomes more wonderful to us, we become more full of wonder that He not only loves us, but that He also *chooses* to love us! At this point we can choose to be overwhelmed with shame, over inflated with pride, or overcome with gratitude. The first option will cause us to resist God. The second will cause God to resist us. But the third...will *transform* us!

REFLECTION

I can't say I'm completely comfortable with knowing that I have crossed the divide between "young man" and, well, the guy I am now. What I find most unnerving about aging is that it doesn't happen with your permission or within your control. Time takes its toll on you stealthily, prompting elastic musculature to pack its bags and whisper to quite a few of the hairs on your head, "The achy joints and the grays have arrived. Our work is done here." And so youth creeps out of you, its departure muffled by the thunderous footfalls of adulthood's tireless companions, *Obligation* and *Responsibility*. Nobody leaves you so much as a Post-It Note. The mirror is the only one kind enough (or cruel enough) to break the news to you that age is setting in. As time continues to steal features and faculties from you, your reflection continues to report it. It doesn't lie to you, and it won't let anyone else lie to you. It keeps an accurate account of your relationship with time.

Spiritually speaking, our reflection keeps an accurate account of our relationship with God. Every encounter with God is documented in our reflection. How we appear spiritually tells others (and ourselves) about how well we're getting along with Him. Over time, laughter, a healthy diet, smoking, exercise, stress, alcohol, and drugs tell their tales on the body, depending on how we live. Likewise, faith, fear, bitterness, joy, contentment, peace, pride, and anger will imprint the spirit, depending on our relationship with God.

> REFLECTION IS GOD'S WAY OF TELLING US THAT HE IS AT WORK IN US.

Reflection is God's way of telling us that He is at work in us. It is confirmation that He has entered the door we opened and has consented to sup with us. *Relationship* is when we come to know a person better. When we *reflect* a person, we have decided that they are worth emulating. God is perfect, which means we're not in relationship with Him for Him to become more like us, but for us to become more like Him (which is His signal that the relationship is working).

Revelation says, "I see."

Recognition says, "I see God."

Relationship declares, "I see God with me."

Reflection shouts, "I see God *in me!*"

Reflection on God produces His glory in us. And because God's glory is always greater than we are, any exposure to it, and expression of it, expands us and changes us. This reflection becomes a new revelation of Him to us, and the cycle of revelation, recognition, relationship, and reflection begins anew on another level.

As God becomes more visible *to* us, He also becomes more visible *in* us. Then we live out the goal of the cycle, which is to participate in the divine nature even as we are transformed to express it. In 2 Corinthians 3:18, Paul called this *"being transformed from glory to glory."* In Psalm 84:7, man is said to go from *"strength to strength."* And in Romans 1:17, the righteousness of God is said to be unveiled *"from faith to faith."* Each of these phrases suggests the results of progressive exposure to the things of God.

Not surprisingly, our own physical anatomy reveals this same pattern. We wouldn't give a newborn a fifty-pound dumbbell to lift; he couldn't handle the weight—he can't even raise his bottle to his mouth. But after he has grown a little more and developed some muscles and coordination, the baby-turned-young man will be able to lift that dumbbell and eventually more. The more we grow, the more we're able to do. The same principle holds true in our developing fellowship with God.

A MODEL OF PERFECTION

For by thy words thou shalt be justified, and by thy words thou shalt be condemned. (Matthew 12:37)

As a pastor, I will have to stand before God one day and give an account of the men and women who have been left in my care. God will look at my congregation and examine their hearts to see if the Word He entrusted to me found its way there; and if it has, He will check to see if it was watered and watched to the best of my ability. As a preacher and teacher, I expect to be held responsible for studying to show myself approved before God, and for communicating to my flock what I learned—not just in word, but also in deed.

The Lord's accounting will include more than just the membership of Faithful Central Bible Church in Los Angeles. It also will include those pastors who fall under my supervision as presiding bishop of the Macedonia International Bible Fellowship. And if I consider what Christ told the Pharisees, then it will even extend to the people who read my books and listen to my tapes.

As I preach, teach, lead, and watch over the people I have been blessed to shepherd, I walk a kind of spiritual tightrope. I am called to watch over the people of God, but those people are not *my* possession, they're God's. I'm just a steward. I never want to stand before God one day and be accused of stealing His property. As a preacher, I want people to listen to me, but I want them to *hear God*. As a teacher, I want people to understand, but I want their understanding to go beyond my words to what *God* is saying to them. There's a thin line between *following* me (the person, the pastor) and following *me* (my behavior).

At times, I have wished I was not accountable for the people of God, because of a very real danger for any pastor who takes his call seriously: the risk of producing good clones instead of good Christians. It's easy to fall into the trap of being satisfied as long as our congregation comes to church every Sunday, listens, shouts, dances, and gives, and then goes home without our checking to see if they have a personal relationship with God that doesn't require a pastor as a go-between. Pastors can become so busy with carrying crippled people to God that they aren't able to carry the healing Word of God to the crippled.

> AS A PREACHER, I WANT PEOPLE TO LISTEN TO ME, BUT I WANT THEM TO HEAR GOD.

If we're not careful, we'll be judged for trying to create God in our own image instead of allowing God to recreate us in His image.

Every once in awhile, I have to remind people that my arms can hug them, but, unlike God's arms, they can't save them. My eyes don't see the deep pain in their heart; and even if I could see it, I can't make them whole again the way a mere glance from the Lord can. From time to time I have to remind myself that I didn't climb up on a cross and die, so I can't keep people out of hell. And I certainly can't be counted on to be sinless, sacrificial, or selfless all the time—I won't even come close. I am as reliant on God's touch of mercy as everyone else. Because I'm not God, I will leave you. Because I'm not Christ, I will forsake you. I'm not the only one who has looked for salvation in things and people rather than in God.

As we focus on the physical image of almighty God, consider the loving kindness that placed the miraculous image of Him right *on* you and *in* you. He did that so we will know that He will never be further from us than we are from Him. He wants us to study Him up close and personal. He wants to teach us what it means to live, to move, and to be in Him, by living, moving, and being in us.

In seeking to understand the anatomy of God, we will find that whenever He shows us anything about His person, we are also given insight into His personality. Since God is a Spirit, the reason He wants to show Himself to us physically is to help us get a handle on His nature. That's why what we will see and learn about God's anatomy is as significant as what we won't. We won't see, for example, the knees of God or the legs of God. Knees or kneeling in Scripture depict submission, fear, begging, or worship. None of these are God's qualities or behavior.

> WHENEVER GOD SHOWS US ANYTHING ABOUT HIS PERSON, WE ARE ALSO GIVEN INSIGHT INTO HIS PERSONALITY.

Despite instances where we read of people "walking" with God, we don't find actual references to "the legs of God" in Scripture. This is because legs appear in the Bible as an image of human strength, and Psalm 147:10 says that God *"taketh not pleasure in the legs of a man,"* meaning He's not impressed with man's power. Legs also move us from one place to another and figuratively represent our way of life, lived out day to day. But God doesn't move from one place to another. He is omnipresent—in all places at all times at the same time. He is eternally self-existent, living outside of time. His life doesn't unfold or "happen" the way ours does; He just *is*.

Shoulders represent labor, or work. God ceased from His creative labors after six days, so we won't find the shoulders of God pictured in Scripture.

The neck is used to reference servitude, submission, or complete subjection. God is God, and beside Him there is none other. He reigns supreme above all things, always. The neck also illustrates the inward inclination of the heart. In the Bible, Israel is continually referred to as a *"stiffnecked people,"* an allusion to their hearts, which were resistant to the things of God.

Presenting our back to another person means we are rejecting them. Because we serve a God who has said He would never leave or forsake us, we won't see Him showing us His back.[1] The Bible speaks of Israel's King Jeroboam casting God behind his back—the ultimate rebuff—and of Israel doing the same with His statutes (1 Kings 14:9, Nehemiah 9:26, and Ezekiel 23:35). That is something we never see God doing—except when it comes to His forgiving our sins (Isaiah 38:17).

We humans are prone to seeing all things from a very egocentric perspective. God knows this, or He would not make the effort to paint a picture of Himself on the canvas we spend the most time looking at: ourselves. It is my hope that this book will be a reminder that He is, and will always be, our only Hero. My prayer is that it will reveal God to you in a way that will confront you, challenge you, and change you.

---

[1] Moses saw God's *"back parts"* as He passed by, but that was to spare Moses certain death at facing God's holiness head-on (Exodus 33:20–23). Only Jesus has beheld God fully, according to John, who proclaimed in his gospel that the Son exists *"in the bosom of the Father"* (John 1:18).

One day we will each stand before Him to account for our time here on Earth, and the only question that will concern Him on that day will be this: *Do you look like Me?* If we have been diligent to read the love letter He has penned to us on the parchment of our own fallible and fault-ridden frames, we will rejoice to answer Him. If we will stop wondering what God has to say on Earth about us, and start seeking out what we have to say on Earth about Him, then our vanity will not have been in vain.

If all you learn from this book is that you were made for God's pleasure and not He for yours, then you will have learned much. And what an amazing thing it will be to know that *you please God!*

As God reveals to you His spectacular physical image, you will discover the glory of His awesome love for you. You will discover that He is not hiding from you. In fact, you were made to come looking for Him.

> *They should seek the Lord, if haply they might feel after him, and find him, though he be not far from every one of us.* (Acts 17:27)

Come with me, and let us seek the image of God...

TWO

TO SEE YOU SMILE: THE FACE OF GOD

"A kindergarten teacher told everyone to draw a picture of what was important to them. In the back of the room Johnny began to labor over his drawing. Everybody else finished and handed in their picture, but he didn't. He was still drawing. The teacher graciously walked back and put her arm around Johnny's shoulder and said, 'Johnny, what are you drawing?' He didn't look up; he just kept on working feverishly at his picture. He said, 'God.' 'But Johnny,' she said gently, 'no one knows what God looks like.' He answered, 'They will when I'm through.'"
—Em Griffin, *The Mind Changers*

My wife, Togetta, is one of the most beautiful women I know. I admit, I am biased. She is my wife, and I love her dearly. Being biased, though, doesn't make me blind. She really is fine. Some people say that when you've been married for many years, you stop seeing your spouse with your eyes and start seeing them with your heart. That's sweet, but praise God, after twenty-five years, my eyes are still happy! In fact, it's a good thing she's my wife, because if she wasn't, I'd get in a lot of trouble for looking at her the way I do!

She has a wonderful face. Like most husbands, I like it more when she's smiling—and I like it even more when I'm the reason she's smiling. In a room crowded with people, I find myself looking for her for no other reason than just to see her face. I don't look longingly into her eyes. I don't hear a symphony and weave my way through a sea of bodies for the touch of her hand. I simply see her, and she sees me see her, and we share a beautiful moment. But I'm not satisfied until her *face* comes into view. It's not enough to see the back of her head or the outline of her frame.

> THE FACE IS WHAT WE REMEMBER MOST AND WHAT WE BELIEVE FIRST ABOUT ANOTHER PERSON.

There is something about a face that connects us to people in ways no other part of the anatomy does. Intimate partners and strangers alike depend on its expression and impression to initiate, enrich, and punctuate every kind of communication. The face is what we remember most and what we believe first about another person. If I tell you I've missed you, my face can make it a lie. If I declare that my heart is broken, my anguished expression confirms my spoken pain. The face is the body's chief instrument of self-expression. We are, for better or worse, our face.

That all may seem elementary until you begin to consider the face of God. What was your first impression of God? Did you imagine that His face looked like holiness? Was His expression one of omniscience or righteousness? Did you see peace when you caught a glimpse of Him? What did your mental image of God's face tell you about how He was feeling? Was He happy? You don't know, do you? We cannot know, because God Himself said in Exodus that no man can see His face and live.

So why are there so many references to *the face of God* in Scripture? And why does God tell us in Psalm 105:4 to *"seek his face"*? Obviously, God wants to reveal something about Himself to us through our understanding of the expression, appearance, and operation of the face.

The movie *Shrek* was an amazing accomplishment in animation. The makers of the film took great pride in the effort that went into making the characters appear more "alive" than they ever had up to that point in the genre. It was interesting to find out that, in the title character, animators working with computers had more than three hundred points of movement in the face alone! In other words, human faces are so complex in the way they move that in order for Shrek's face to appear as "human" as possible, the artists and engineers had to manipulate its movement in more than three hundred different places. Can you point to several *hundred* places on your face? Probably not. And that gives us an idea of how truly complex the face is.

It's the same with God. All God is, resides in His face. Therefore, to "seek His face" is to seek to *see* Him. However, since we can't actually *see* God, He must have had something else in mind when He told us to seek Him and promised He'd be found. *Seeking the face of God* has a number of connotations. First and most obvious is the idea of seeking an audience with God. David called this *inquiring of God in His temple.* The temple of God is anywhere God's presence resides. Therefore, to

37

seek God's presence is to go to God's house to spend time with Him.

TO SEEK HIS FACE

Several passages in Scripture illuminate the idea of *the face of God*, which is referred to throughout the Bible. The book of Psalms probably presents the most vivid personal images of man's search for God. The Psalms spread before us a glorious portrait of the multifaceted nature of God, and an exquisite rendering of His face in particular.

> *The LORD is my light and my salvation; whom shall I fear? the LORD is the strength of my life; of whom shall I be afraid?...For in the time of trouble he shall hide me in his pavilion: in the secret of his tabernacle shall he hide me; he shall set me up upon a rock. And now shall mine head be lifted up above mine enemies round about me: therefore will I offer in his tabernacle sacrifices of joy; I will sing, yea, I will sing praises unto the LORD. Hear, O LORD, when I cry with my voice: have mercy also upon me, and answer me. When thou saidst, Seek ye my face, my heart said unto thee, Thy face, LORD, will I seek. Hide not thy face far from me; put not thy servant away in anger: thou hast been my help; leave me not, neither forsake me, O God of my salvation.*
>
> (Psalm 27:1, 5–9)

In the above psalm, God told David to seek His face. That in itself is a revelation of the will of God: He *desires* that you and I be anxious to see His face. In Psalm 27:7, David said that when he calls on God, he wants the Lord to have mercy upon him. When we seek to be with God, we automatically need mercy because, as we've learned, the Bible says no man will see the face of God and live.

To See You Smile: The Face of God

But if that's so, then why, in Genesis 33:10, was Jacob stunned at having *"seen the face of God"* and not struck dead? Because Jacob didn't see God's actual naked face—he couldn't live through that. In actuality, the face of God, the essence of the glory of God, was filtered through His love and mercy. In other words, the full radiance of God's face was covered in a sheath of His kindness and grace. God's mercy is in effect twenty-four hours a day, seven days a week, fifty-two weeks a year, because He *wants* us to seek His face, and He wants us to survive the experience.

To "seek" means *to have a sincere desire* for something. In this context it means one sincerely wants an audience with God. That's why, when God told the psalmist to seek Him, the response was, "My heart said, 'I will seek Your face.'" God doesn't want us to seek Him unless we want to. He's not looking for "Curious George." He doesn't want "lookie-loos" with "drive-by devotion," who're just checking in to say a quick "Hey!" and shout a loud "Amen!" The seekers God is seeking are the ones who have a sincere desire in their hearts to *find* Him.

> GOD'S MERCY IS IN EFFECT TWENTY-FOUR HOURS A DAY.

Psalm 24 gives us other requirements for seeking an audience with God. That psalm is part of a group of psalms called "Psalms of Ascent," which are songs designated to be sung when the people of God went up to the temple or to Jerusalem to worship God. In Israel today, there is a hilltop upon which rests the remains of one wall of the ancient temple. Coming up out of a valley are steps that lead up to that wall. In order to come up to the temple, the worshippers would walk—sometimes by the thousands—from all over the known world, through the valley, to the foot of the mountain. There they stopped and performed a ritual of praise.

Here's the scene: The people are on their way to the temple to commune with God, to be with God, to seek His face. They come through the valley and stop at the base of the mountain, and a priest says:

> *Who shall ascend into the hill of the* LORD*? or who shall stand in his holy place?* (Psalm 24:3)

In a sort of "call and response," another priest would sing the next verse:

> *He that hath clean hands, and a pure heart; who hath not lifted up his soul unto vanity, nor sworn deceitfully.*
> (Psalm 24:4)

After they make that declaration, the worshipper would ascend the steps, up into the temple, and into the presence (or "the face") of God. Hence the designation "Psalms of Ascent."

There is another requirement for the believer who would seek the face of God. Who will ascend into the presence of God? Who will be allowed to see His face? He who has clean hands and a pure heart! At this point, many people would just excuse themselves and say to the priests, "Fellows, you all head on up the stairs without me now. I'll be waiting here when you get back." However, *"clean hands, and a pure heart"* is not a declaration of one's righteousness. It is a declaration of a *sincere desire* for righteousness. Righteousness itself was not the requirement to enter into the presence of God; otherwise no one could ever enter into His presence. The requirement for being in God's presence was a spoken desire for the resulting righteousness that comes from being in the presence of God.

Verse six of the same psalm says that those who truly desire to come into the presence of God do come into His presence and thereby do have their hands and hearts cleansed. It reveals and acknowledges God's standard. But it also speaks to the fact that we cannot meet God's standard all by ourselves. We need God Himself to produce that standard in us, because we don't have clean hands and a pure heart. But as we seek His face and He allows us into His presence by His mercy, then we get our hands cleaned and our heart purified. Thus, being "clean and pure" are not requirements to get into His presence nor do they indicate perfection, but rather they are results of *being* in His presence.

To *see the face of God* is to have an audience with Him so He can remind us of the call upon our lives: to have clean hands and a pure heart—"being righteous before God." Being right before God is always the combination of what's inside *and* what's outside. Clean hands outside; pure heart inside.

MANY PEOPLE SET THEIR STANDARDS BY WATCHING OTHER PEOPLE'S BEHAVIOR.

Righteousness is a life of integrity and character. Character before men, and integrity before God. Righteousness is not only what we do internally, it's also how we live our life externally, in accordance with God's standard.

Many people set their standards by watching other people's behavior. Their concern is not how clean their own hands are, but only that they are cleaner than the next person's. But

41

since everyone's hands are dirty, nobody is clean—not one of us is perfect.

God is concerned not only with how we talk, but with how we walk. Not only with what we think, but with what we do. Not only with what we believe, but with how we behave. Not only with our principles, but with our practices. Not only with what we know, but with whether we *act* on what we know.

And He is not just thinking about our own personal hands and heart; He is also concerned about the generations:

This is the generation of them that seek him. (Psalm 24:6)

God does not allow you into His presence to teach you, bless you, and change you just for you alone. His concern is for you, your children, your grandchildren, and your great-grandchildren. He looks for *generations* who will seek Him.

We live in a society that is consumed with itself. People live in bondage to materialism and secularism, because they have not been taught to seek and prioritize the things of God. But if we would only make God our priority and seek an audience with Him, then He will show us how to live our lives for Him, and how to raise generations who will do the same.

KNOWING HIS ASSISTANCE: "THE SEQUENCE OF DAVID"

Seek the LORD, and his strength: seek his face evermore.
(Psalm 105:4)

To seek the face of God is to have His assistance. Psalm 105 implies that there is a relationship between the face of God and the strength of God. His face is related to His help, His empowerment, and His aid. When we come into His presence, we understand that what He requires of us cannot be done in our own strength. I can't live the way God wants me to live by my own wisdom and understanding. In fact, one writer in Proverbs cautioned us not to live by our own understanding but by the assistance and guidance of the Lord. It is as we seek His face that His face gives us a revelation of His strength.

Psalm 27:8 finds the writer promising to seek God's face. The next verse says, *"Hide not thy face far from me."* From this, we learn that the God who can reveal His face can also hide it. Probably one of the best ways to understand the assistance and strength of God in the context of seeking the face of God is to look at what happens when His face is not there. There is good news and bad news on that front. The bad news is, God can hide His face from us! The good news is...God can hide His face from us. That may sound a bit schizophrenic, but we humans some-times do a little flip-flop when it comes

> TO SEEK THE FACE OF GOD IS TO HAVE HIS ASSISTANCE.

to the idea of the face of God: We flip out when He gets too far into our business, our marriage, our finances, and our rela-tionships. If He shines too much light on us, He becomes the unwelcome guest. Then, when we flop out there in the world all by ourselves, we suddenly want Him to come near us!

In Psalm 51, we learn about King David's sin before God. This is his psalm of repentance. David says in Psalm 51:9, *"Hide thy face from my sins, and blot out all mine iniquities."* This is the same David of Psalm 27 whose heart told God he would seek Him, but here he is asking God to hide His face from his sins!

I know how David must have felt. Have you ever done anything or saw something in yourself about which you wanted to say, "Lord, don't look at that"? We've all had things going on that we wanted to hide and cover up because we didn't want God to see them. Have you ever tried to sweep something under the carpet while you were praying? We figure if we don't mention it, then maybe God won't know about it, or maybe He'll just let it slide. But that's not how God works. If you are dealing with a sin that you haven't quite gotten a handle on and you ask God not to look at it, you are actually asking Him not to look at *you*—much like a child caught in the act of doing something he knows he shouldn't and immediately turning away so he can't see your face. We mustn't be too quick to ask God not to look at something, because we are, in effect, asking Him to turn His face away from us.

We should never want God to hide His face from us. Sure, it's tough to face Him sometimes, because when He faces our sin, He has to deal with us on it. But if He ever does turn His face from us, we're stuck with our sin and without our God. And that's a truly tight spot to be in.

So in Psalm 27 David said he would seek God's face, and in Psalm 51 he says, "Don't look—hide Your face from my sin." Now look at what he says in Psalm 30:

> *I will extol thee, O LORD; for thou hast lifted me up, and hast not made my foes to rejoice over me. O LORD my God, I cried unto thee, and thou hast healed me. O LORD, thou hast brought up my soul from the grave: thou hast kept me alive, that I should not go down to the pit. Sing unto the LORD, O ye saints of his, and give thanks at the remembrance of his holiness. For his anger endureth but a moment; in his favour is life: weeping may endure for a night, but joy cometh in the morning.* (Psalm 30:1–5)

David is giving testimony; all is well. Now the next verse:

And in my prosperity I said, I shall never be moved.

(Psalm 30:6)

In effect, he is saying, "After You bless me, 'I can handle it from there.'" David was dancing and singing and praising the Lord for hearing his cry, delivering him, healing him, getting him out of a pit, making his enemies leave him alone, helping him through his dark nights of weeping. And then, in his prosperity, he decided that things were okay! God can clock out now, take a break, go on back up to heaven! David is basically saying, "Good job, God! I'll call You if I need You again."

Then comes the next verse:

Thou didst hide thy face, and I was troubled. (Psalm 30:7)

After his success, David got grand. After his blessing, healing, and rescue, he decided he could handle things by himself and take on the mountains. The Lord had set him up. As soon as David said, "I shall not be moved," God moved! He hid His face from David, and David was sorely troubled! We humans do flip-flop, don't we.

There's a dramatic Hebrew picture word for "trouble." It means *to be in a tight place.* When God hides His face, He hides His assistance and His strength; and that puts us in a tight place—in a "jam." We can't turn and run because we can't turn in a tight place. Sometimes our place can get so tight that we can't even put our arms up. All we can do is holler, "Hey, Lord, help!—look this way, please!"

When God turns His face away, He's doing more than not looking in your direction. He's ignoring you. He has broken off communication with you. He has withdrawn His favor. When you call on Him, He acts as though He can't hear you. Your prayers hit the ceiling and go no higher. Have you ever been in a situation in which you felt like you couldn't even get in touch with God? Some of us have been in some tight places with God. Some of us have made some wrong turns, blown it, followed the wrong person, went down the wrong path, and gotten so far away from God that we felt we couldn't even call on Him. All we could do was hope that God would mercifully look our way, because we realize that when He hid His face from us, we were in big trouble. For some of us, God needs to hide His face so we'll wake up.

So here's the sequence of David:

Psalm 27, *"I will seek Your face."*

Psalm 51, *"Lord, don't look this way—hide Your face."*

Psalm 30, *"When You hid Your face, I was troubled."*

Now let's go to Psalm 69:17: *"And hide not thy face from thy servant; for I am in trouble: hear me speedily."* I love that verse! "Please, Lord, don't hide Your face from Your servant"—oh, now he's a servant! If I were God, I'd say, "Make up your mind! What do you want Me to do already?" We get real grand sometimes, don't we. Then, when we get in a mess, we get all humble. "Hello, Lord? Begging Your pardon, Almighty. It's Your lowly servant here, Father. Remember me? Please don't hide Your face from me." I love the Word of God. Look at the sequence:

"I will seek Your face, Lord."

"Lord, hide Your face."

"When You hid Your face, I was in trouble."

"Lord, please don't hide Your face. I'm in trouble over here!"

To See You Smile: The Face of God

When our sin causes God to turn His face from us, He may withdraw His covering, or lift His favor; but He never forsakes us. His turning away is a response to our forsaking Him.

Keep On Shining

And the LORD spake unto Moses, saying, Speak unto Aaron and unto his sons, saying, On this wise ye shall bless the children of Israel, saying unto them, The LORD bless thee, and keep thee: the LORD make his face shine upon thee, and be gracious unto thee: the LORD lift up his countenance upon thee, and give thee peace.   (Numbers 6:22–26)

When God *lifts up His countenance* upon you, it means He's smiling. I want to make God smile. I want to live my life in such a way that when He looks into my life, He smiles. His smile indicates His pleasure and His acceptance. Have you ever considered just how much is communicated by a smile? Parents who are really wired to their children don't have to use a lot of words. Sometimes a parent at the bedside of a suffering child will muster up all the strength he or she has and smile, and that baby knows that everything will be all right. There's something about mommy's or daddy's smile that chases fear away. There's something about the smile you get from your children. There's something about my wife's smile. And there's really something about God's smile!

"May the Lord make His face to shine upon you" refers to the favor of God. When His face shines on your business, it means that your business has the favor of God on it. When God makes His face to shine on your home, your family is covered by favor.

"Shine" literally speaks of the shining of the sun. Notice that God makes His face *shine*. This is an act of His will that is preceded by a desire in our heart. When we desire to seek His face, it is a choice our heart makes; and then God reveals to us His face, shining upon us. He chooses to flash His light in our direction when we seek His direction. So, for example, the blessing God gave to Moses for His children, "May God's mercy and favor radiate in your life," is a declaration of a desire for us to know that we are accepted in the face of God and that His acceptance will be visible.

God's face is always shining. He doesn't start shining, stop shining, and start shining again. It's like the sun: God's shining never goes out!

> LIKE THE SUN, GOD'S SHINING NEVER GOES OUT!

Verse twenty-six adds to the blessing by pronouncing, "[May] *the* LORD *lift up his countenance upon thee.*" This is likened to the rising of the sun. The idea of the sun rising implies that while it is always shining, we don't always see it. We will go through seasons when we cannot see the glow on the face of God; not necessarily because God is angry with us, but because there are times when we simply can't see Him. Just because it's nighttime, does not mean the sun stopped shining; it's just shining in a different hemisphere of the world.

Sometimes in our spiritual walk it will get dark. It doesn't matter how big our Bible is or how sweetly we sing in church. It doesn't matter how pretty our prayers are, how long we've been saved, how well we speak in tongues, or how much Scripture we can quote. Sometimes it will just get dark, because nighttime always comes.

To See You Smile: The Face of God

Nighttime is not always comfortable, but it is necessary. Nighttime is that time in your spiritual walk when everything you know to be true about God is put to the test. You will be tried and stretched during your nighttime. You will weep, as David did. You will not see the face of God. But simply trust that He has not forsaken you. Don't lose heart in the nighttime, for as surely as nighttime comes, eventually it goes. Since God created the world, morning has followed evening. We just have to wait it out, and the sun will rise again. It does not matter how strong the storm is; if you can just hold on through the night, the light will come. It does not matter how dreary it is. It doesn't matter how bad things look. Just hold on. Alone or in a crowd, hold on. Your night might be a little longer than somebody else's—you might be in one of those Alaska nights that seem to go on forever—but simply trust the faithfulness of the sun, for it never fails to rise on schedule.

> **Nighttime is not always comfortable, but it is necessary.**

When God does shine His face on your life, some folks ask the wrong question. They ask what God looked like when you saw His face. The question is not what God looked like; the question is "What did you look like after you saw Him?" Moses went to the top of Mount Sinai and saw the face of God (which was not the raw, unshielded glory of God, but His glory draped by the fragrance of His love), and when he came down from that mountain, the Bible says, *"His face shone"* (Exodus 34:29). Wow! When God shines on us, He makes *us* shine!

Have you ever hugged somebody so close that their makeup rubbed off on you? One day my wife kissed me, and

49

shortly after that, I entered a room where some other people were. A couple of them saw her lipstick and figured they'd do me a favor and wipe it off. I wouldn't let them. I did not want my wife's kiss wiped off of me, because it brings memories of a pleasant experience.

When you come into the presence of the living God and He smiles on you, some of His shine rubs off on you, and even after you go about the rest of your business, you keep on shining. You may have come into His presence without a dime in your pocket, but you shine, dear child of God! You're struggling and being stretched, but you're still shining! You may be all by yourself in your situation, but you keep on shining!

May the Lord bless you and keep you. May He make
His face to shine upon you and be gracious unto you.
May you always see God's dazzling smile.

THREE

THE EVER WATCHING EYES OF GOD

When I panic, I run.
When I run, I lose.
When I lose, God waits.
When I wait, He fights.
When He fights, I learn.
—Charles Swindoll, *The Tale of the Tardy Oxcart*

On September 11, 2001, a blade of terrorism maliciously sliced through the seemingly flawless features of America's composure. Much has been written and spoken about the thousands who died, the millions still in mourning, and so many heroes who were shaped, refined, and defined by that international calamity.

One question has plagued me since that day: "God...did You *see* that?"

I don't want to know anything else. I don't need to know why all those children had to lose their parents. It grieves me, but I don't have to know why. To be honest, I'm having a hard enough time trying to deal with today. Yesterday somebody opened an envelope laced with Anthrax, and today he's dead. Today there was another terrorist threat. Today twenty thousand men and women lost their jobs. Today is consuming me. Tomorrow is too much for me to think about at the moment. But I have to know, for my sanity, for my peace of mind, "Lord, did You see that?" ...Did He *see* it?

I grapple with that question. I wrestle with it and struggle with it, and soon I realize that I'm not the only one holding on in this fight. That question has gripped me as tightly as I have gripped it. God has been waiting for us to ask that question. He has been waiting for us to ask the obvious, the question only a child would ask.

> GOD REVEALS HIMSELF WITHIN THE CONFINES OF HUMAN INTELLECT AND UNDERSTANDING.

The eyes of God aren't a debatable issue for us believers. We know God has eyes. He had to be able to see to create the world and run the universe. But what does that really mean? Blind people have eyes. People who wear glasses have eyes. Someone who avoids you has eyes. People who are sleeping have eyes. What does it mean to say that *God has eyes*? Does He see you?

When we consider the concept of *the eyes of God*, we need to understand that God doesn't have eyeballs: He sees *spiritually*. His eyes are as spirit as He is. Our eyes take in light, shape, and depth in various forms, and we process that information in our brain. Our brain tells us what we're looking at, and it is at that point that we "see." God's eyes *see*—period. His eyes are not like ours. His eyes look, process, and know, all at the same time. God doesn't have to think about what He sees. He doesn't have to turn it upside down and inside out to get a thorough understanding of it. He knew everything about it long before the instant He saw it.

THE EVER WATCHING EYES OF GOD

Since God reveals Himself to us within the confines of human intellect and understanding, we're going to explore His eyes within the context of the mechanics of human vision. Because God looks, processes, and understands at the moment He sees, then *"the eyes of God"* refer to His *omniscience*. God doesn't see just the physical properties of something He's looking at; He sees the intellectual, spiritual, and social properties as well. He also knows how what He is looking at relates to the world it is in and the people around it and how it will impact (and be impacted by) all things and all people in the *future*! All that and more are involved in God's visual faculties.

I will use three broad categories in dealing with the eyes of God:

How He sees us.

How He looks at us.

How He looks for us.

The order may seem backward, since we usually look *for* something first, then look *at* it, and then really *see* it. But with God, there is comfort in knowing that He *sees* us, there is responsibility in knowing that He looks *at* us, and there is security in knowing that He looks *for* us. Personally, I'd rather have the comfort of God's closeness, and then work my way out to feeling secure when He seems far away, because I need to know that He sees me.

EYES THAT SEE ME

In the LORD put I my trust: how say ye to my soul, Flee as a bird to your mountain? For, lo, the wicked bend their bow, they make ready their arrow upon the string, that they may privily shoot at the upright in heart....The LORD is in his holy temple, the LORD's throne is in heaven: his eyes behold, his eyelids try, the children of men. (Psalm 11:1–2, 4)

Obviously, the God who sees is all-knowing. In Scripture, there are many references to idol gods and the people who worship handmade statues that "have eyes but cannot see." Man makes these little deities and puts eyes on them; but Scripture says their eyes cannot see. When man makes an idol, it is his attempt to make God in his own image. To say that the idol can't see is an amplification of that truth since only a man who is blind to the presence of God would craft an idol and hold it up before God Himself.

David, however, declared the truth about the almighty and eternal God, by saying that we serve and worship a God who doesn't just have eyes, but whose eyes actually *see*. The psalm above is a vivid illustration of the operation of the eyes of God and how they see. First of all, the psalmist shows us that God can see us in the context of trials: The wicked were getting ready to shoot at David. The *New King James Version* uses the word *"secretly"*; another version says *"privily"*; still another says *"in darkness."* The idea is that there was a climate of fear, frustration, and hopelessness. The situation was a grave one for David, the conquering king of Israel. Many scholars believe that he was on the run when this text was written. Some believe he was running from Saul, who was out to kill him. Others think this psalm was penned in that season when he was running from his own son Absalom. Whatever the case, it is clear that David was under attack. He was going through something he identified as *the enemy,* who was aiming bows and arrows at him and attacking him in the darkness.

David wasn't paranoid, he was afraid. This was a bad situation—people were after him who wanted to see him *dead*. It can be argued that the mention of bows and arrows is significant in this context because they can be weapons of a terrorist since they can shoot at their target or adversary without actually coming face to face with him. There's some support for this in the text, because the enemy mentioned was trying to wage his battle *"secretly."*

> **DARKNESS MEANS YOU DON'T KNOW WHO THE ENEMY IS.**

David was being attacked by an enemy he couldn't see, and being shot at with arrows he couldn't see. He was in the dark, the enemy was in the dark, and the arrows were in the dark. Have you ever been under attack like that? It's bad enough to have an enemy, but darkness throws a few other factors into the mix. Darkness means you don't know who the enemy is, what they look like, how close they are, and whether or not they are moving around you. Darkness cloaks the direction and size of the arrows. You're in a stressful, dangerous situation. You want to defend yourself, but you can't see what you're defending yourself from!

David painted the picture of a God who can see you in your temptation. The temptation identified in the passage is subtle but unmistakable: The enemy was attacking him in the darkness, and out of that darkness a voice spoke and said, *"Flee as a bird to your mountain."* Temptation will most likely raise its head in the midst of a trial. The voice told David,

"Get out of here! There's no way out of this—you can't defeat this enemy! *Run!*" A climate of fear and uncertainty often comes during trials.

David said, "*You* say to me." Who is "you"? There are several options. "You" could be the enemy—the one who wants to destroy you is telling you to run to the mountains. The problem with that scenario is that in battle, particularly in the part of the country David was in, the enemy often lurked in the mountains. It would have been to the enemy's advantage to have David run somewhere away from familiarity and into his grasp. Have you ever been faced with a dilemma and realized that if you make one misstep, your situation will go from bad to worse? If it is the enemy tempting you to run in your trial, then you can be certain that his plan is to turn you away from God and into his hands!

> SOMETIMES WE TELL OURSELVES THAT HOLINESS IS TOO HIGH A PRICE TO PAY.

Then, the "you" could have been God Himself. There are legitimate times when God tells us to run. It would not be out of His character to instruct us to do that; not necessarily because we can't handle a situation, but because our deliverance might be in another place. If we stay where we are, we may miss a blessing. It may not be God's plan for you to stay where you are. When God tells you to run, it may be to keep you from falling into some sin that you might be helpless against. Remember Joseph? When Potiphar's wife laid her filthy hands on Joseph, the Bible says that Joseph *fled!* He ran so fast he left his clothes in the woman's hands! Sometimes it's better to be naked and publicly embarrassed than be fully clothed and ashamed before God.

Another possibility is that the "you" could be well-meaning friends. Sometimes, people who genuinely care about us will observe our situation and determine (often without checking with God) that we can't handle it and that it makes good sense for us to run. Unfortunately, good sense isn't always God sense. They may have decided that you need to run because they were in the same situation once, and they ran. Or they imagine that they would run if they were in those circumstances. But we do not live by the wisdom of men.

Finally, the "you" could simply be *you*. David could have been talking to himself. Have you ever tried to talk yourself out of staying in a bad situation, explaining to yourself that you shouldn't have to endure the hardship or pain of it? Have you ever sat down and carefully created a handwritten, monogrammed, personally engraved invitation to your own private pity party? You invited yourself as the guest of honor. You danced with yourself, talked to yourself, and told yourself how bad things are, and then you told yourself you shouldn't have to take it. Outraged, you told yourself, "You need to leave that mess—man, you oughta run!" And you agreed with yourself and ran.

Sometimes we tell ourselves that holiness is too high a price to pay. It's too lonely being chaste. We ought to run. Sometimes that voice tells us that the boss won't notice if a few things are missing. In other words, we ought to run from our integrity. Has a voice ever told you to run from the loneliness of being the only Christian where you work?

His Light in our Darkness

God sees us in our trials. He also sees us in our darkest hours:

If I say, Surely the darkness shall cover me; even the night shall be light about me. Yea, the darkness hideth not from thee; but the night shineth as the day: the darkness and the light are both alike to thee. (Psalm 139:11–12)

There are two things to observe in the above Scripture: First (and most obvious), is that darkness and light don't make any difference to God; He sees with His *Spirit*. Your enemies can hide from you in the dark, but they can't hide from God. Second is that the night becomes light around you. Wait a minute—how does night become light? What turns the lights on in the night seasons of our life? *Faith!* Faith is the divine switch of every believer. Faith comes by hearing, and hearing by the Word of God (Romans 10:17). When you're in the dark, the only thing you have to depend on is what God has already said to you. If He said He would never leave you or forsake you, then He must be with you in the dark as well as the light. If He said no weapon formed against you will prosper, then those arrows in the dark may hit you, but they won't kill you. If He said resist the enemy and he will flee, then you stand there in the dark and call the devil a liar, and he will flee.

The Word of God is a *"lamp unto* [our] *feet and a light unto* [our] *path"* (Psalm 119:105). The Word lights our way in the darkness, but it's very interesting how that works. It doesn't make all things visible to us; it just tells us where everything is. When you're in your darkness, you may not be able to see the enemy, but the Word will give you his coordinates so that you'll know his position in relation to you.

A good analogy is bats. Bats can't see. But if you put them in a room full of furniture, they can fly around all day and never hit anything. That's because they have an unusually keen sense of hearing. Sound waves bounce off everything, and they know by hearing how far away something is, how it's shaped, and what its density is. Likewise, the Spirit of Truth that lives in you (Truth is the Word of God) will bring to your remembrance everything you need to know to make it through the darkness. You may want to give up, but the Word of God says, *"Let patience have her perfect work"* (James 1:4). You may want to panic, but the Word says, "Worry for nothing" (Philippians 4:6). You may think you're alone, but the Word says, "Nothing shall separate you from the love of God" (Romans 8:39). The Word will let you know if you're in the gutter because of your own sin, or if you're in your Gethsemane—a place where God stretches you just before you walk into your destiny. If you will only believe it, the Word makes all things visible to your spirit. Without faith, the Word is just ink on paper.

> WITHOUT FAITH, THE WORD IS JUST INK ON PAPER.

The key to handling trials and temptations is to know that God sees them and that He is not looking at your trial or temptation, He is looking at *you*. He wants to see your *trust* in Him. If He sees that, then He will move mountains for you. The eyes of God, which see everything, can see whether or not you trust Him! The God who sees your trust, saw it before He saw you in the darkness. He allowed the darkness to happen to you so that you'd see what He sees: A person who trusts Him enough to listen for His voice in the darkness; a person who knows how to get to peace in darkness; a person who knows that perfect love casts out fear in the darkness.

David said in Psalm 11:1, *"In the LORD put I my trust."* It's not an accident that those are the very first words of the psalm. Before the trial, before the darkness, before the arrows, before the temptation to run, David put his trust in the Lord! Then he went on to tell how he was being attacked by the enemy. It's like he was trying to make sense of it. He couldn't quite explain it. And in his confusion, he was hearing a voice telling him to run and throw in the towel—*"Flee as a bird?"* (Psalm 11:1).

Does that sequence sound familiar? You put your trust in God, and then the attack comes. You weren't doing so badly out there in the world. Then you decided to put your trust in God. All was wonderful and spiritual and exciting...but then the darkness seemed to come out of nowhere—yet, you had already put your trust in the Lord! It seemed like as soon as you determined that you were going to be holy, all hell broke loose. And that's *exactly* what happened. You didn't think satan was going to give you up without a fight, did you? You didn't think he was going to just sit by and watch you ravage the gates to his kingdom through the power of your ministry, did you? We must never forget that he will try to take you out at every opportunity. But the devil doesn't even know how much God loves you! The eyes of God see you; they see your trials, they see your temptations. But first, they see your trust in *Him*.

HIS EYES BEHOLD ALL

Psalm 11:4 says that God's eyes *"behold."* The tense of the verb makes it more accurately rendered, "His eyes are beholding"—He *is seeing*. He continues to see into our lives, which means that God is not just taking a passing glance at us; He gazes at us. *Gaze* literally means "to cut, dissect, or split." God cuts through all the stuff in your life and His gaze zeroes in on *you*.

The eyelids of God also come into play here. Psalm 11:4 says that the eyelids of God *"try"* men. Picture a person squinting to see something more clearly. God "squints" to focus on the intimate details of your life. His squinting goes into the smallest, darkest, most recessed place in your heart and exposes things in you that even you don't know about.

But why would God, who can see everything, need to squint? God "squinting" His eyes is simply an image to use so we can understand the context of the psalm *and* our circumstances. Squinting gives clarity to things that may be difficult for the human eye to see. We don't squint to see things we don't care about. When God squints at us, He is intensely watching us as we go through a trial, to see if we will come to realize that what we thought was insignificant is actually messing up our lives. The eyelids of God—the *squinting* of God—try men.

Trials are never without a purpose. They always bring up to the surface behaviors, emotions, and habits that hinder our walk with God. You may think that anger against your father is no big deal. In fact, you think you've dealt with it. But God sees a tiny, scared little girl or boy protecting themselves in the corner of their heart. When He squints and allows things to happen that bring pain to the surface of your consciousness, you will see that child, too. Those "little white lies" we tell may not be a big deal to us, but God will allow one of them to try you because He wants to destroy that deceptive, manipulative spirit in us that wars with His nature in us. God doesn't squint so that He can see better; He squints so *we* can see better.

IN *His* IMAGE

The greatest comfort can be found in the image of the eyelids of God. Yes, they test us, and no, it's not always pleasant. But God never puts us through a test He hasn't taught us to pass. Remember, His eyes watch to see if we trust Him. He knows what our trust consists of, so He's not going to test us on anything we haven't yet learned about Him.

When I was in the sixth grade, I had a teacher named Thelma Jean Nickerson. When Ms.

> **TRIALS ARE NEVER WITHOUT A PURPOSE.**

Nickerson gave us a test, she would do two things. First, she would say, "Clear your desk." Then, she would say, "Keep your eyes straight ahead." She'd pass out the tests, then say, "You may begin." And we would turn our papers over and start working. She would sit at her desk and watch us there weeping and gnashing our teeth. We were tortured, feet-tapping, head-scratching, hair-pulling, struggling little balls of anxiety. And she just looked at us with the tiniest smirk on her face that seemed to say, *What are you all waiting for? Hurry up and finish this test so I can go home.*

Then she would do something strange. She would get up and walk up and down the aisles, looking at every student as he or she took the test. To me, she was the meanest woman in the world. But one day, Ms. Nickerson blew my mind. To this day, I haven't forgotten what she did. Ms. Nickerson was walking by my desk during one of her grueling exams, and I was really struggling! I was having a rough time with one particular problem, and it didn't help one bit that Ms. Nickerson kept walking past my desk. I thought to myself, *Is she getting some kinda twisted fun out of watching me sweat like this?!*

THE EVER WATCHING EYES OF GOD

I decided to guess at the answer to the problem I was struggling with. I figured a slim chance was better than none, and I wanted to get her off my back. I didn't know the answer anyway, and it didn't look like it was going to fall out of the sky real soon and plop down onto my desk, so I decided to put a check in a box and get it over with. And then, just as I was about to put a check in the wrong box, Ms. Nickerson silently pointed with her finger at the right answer and kept on going!

To this day I am stunned. If I wasn't so surprised, I could have kissed mean ol' Ms. Nickerson. The woman who gave me the test also gave me the answer to a problem that was stumping me! In that same way, God knows when we're going through a test—He allowed the test to come on us in the first place. And just when we think we can't struggle anymore and we're about to give up, He'll let the Holy Spirit give us the answer. He wants us to know that every test He allows is open-book: The Bible has every answer we will ever need, and we are allowed to use it for everything in life. In fact, we're encouraged to. Only a dummy would go to an open-book test and not bring the book with all the answers!

EYES THAT LOOK AT ME

And the times of this ignorance God winked at; but now commandeth all men every where to repent. (Acts 17:30)

What is in the winking of the eye? Sometimes the wink simply means *I see you.* Sometimes it means *I see you, and I want to see more of you.* Sometimes it means *I saw what you did, and I'm going to act like I didn't see it, but I want you to know that I saw it.*

IN *His* IMAGE

I take a lot of comfort in knowing that God sees me. However, there can also be a lot of discomfort in knowing that. I've done some things I wish God hadn't seen. We saw in the chapter on "The Face of God" that David was bold enough to ask God not to look at some of his behavior. The knowledge that God sees me does not always make me feel warm and fuzzy—mostly because I know that while the loving-kindness of God sees me, so do His eyes of justice and righteousness! So when I sin, I run the risk of offending the holiness of God on a day when His mercy is not as abundant as I would like it to be. That's why it's good to know that while God sees me with His eyes, there are some times when He will merely look at me and not gaze. In those times, He makes it clear that He's not ignoring me or excusing me; He's just cutting me a little slack...*for now.*

> *Then Paul stood in the midst of Mars' hill and said, Ye men of Athens, I perceive that in all things ye are too superstitious. For as I passed by, and beheld your devotions, I found an altar with this inscription,* TO THE UNKNOWN GOD. *Whom therefore ye ignorantly worship, him declare I unto you.*
>
> (Acts 17:22–23)

In Athens, there is a place called Mars Hill, where, long ago, men would engage in philosophical discussion and debate. All the great minds and great thinkers would gather and talk about whatever they wanted to. Mars Hill was known for the high intellectual caliber of its philosophical orators and thinkers. That site is still there today.

One day, the apostle Paul showed up at Mars Hill and spoke. He gave a discourse wherein he proposed to introduce them to the one true and living God. He told them that he had seen an inscription on a plaque that read *To the Unknown God*. Paul offered to introduce the people to this God they did not know. In his speech, he gave a wonderful revelation about the eyes of God:

> *For in him we live, and move, and have our being; as certain also of your own poets have said, For we are also his offspring. Forasmuch then as we are the offspring of God, we ought not to think that the Godhead is like unto gold, or silver, or stone, graven by art and man's device.*
>
> (Acts 17:28–29)

As Paul made his way through the city of Athens, he could not help but notice that the city was filled with idol gods everywhere (even today there are remnants of idols all over the city of Athens). So Paul decided to go to the most public place in this city of idols and preach the Gospel there up on Mars Hill.

He talked about God the Creator, who created us all out of one blood. He talked about unity within humanity and unity of origin. He pointed out that even the Greeks' own poets affirmed that we are God's offspring. By the time Paul got to verses 28 and 29, he was talking about how God is not like gold or silver or stone—something that can be shaped by art and man's devising. Paul declared to them that this *Unknown God* is actually the One in whom we live and move and have our being. He is the God who wants to be known. But He's not a God who was shaped by human hands, because that would make Him mere a human product.

Paul went on to explain that during those times when people were tempted to depict God along with other man-made idols, God mercifully winked at them and chalked it up to their ignorance. When Paul characterized them as ignorant, they would not have taken offense because, remember, these were the great thinkers of Greece: To be ignorant meant simply to be unexposed or uninformed. They were very open to new revelation; ignorance was seen as an opportunity to learn. The Greek word Paul used when he said they were "ignorant" is the same word as the "unknown" that was written in the inscription "To the Unknown God."

HE IS THE GOD WHO WANTS TO BE KNOWN.

He was brilliantly laying out the argument that the Unknown God whom they were building altars to wants to be *known*. But he let them know that God can't be made with human hands.

Paul explained that when the Greeks built their idols, they didn't know that; but God understood that and had been patient with their ignorance because they didn't know any better. In other words, God *"winked"* at their ignorance.

To "wink" means to "overlook." God overlooked the fact that idol worship offended Him. But because of their ignorance, He overlooked it. The word *overlook* means to "look beyond." God saw their ignorance and made note of it, but He chose not to blast them for it, because they had no revelation of Him in their lives yet. However, with the arrival of Paul, that was about to change.

When God winks, or overlooks our sin, that does not imply by any means that He approves of it or ignores it. Many of us conclude that because God overlooked our sin and did nothing, we must have gotten away with something. However, to say that God winked is to say that He did not punish us with the severity that our disobedience warranted. Since

He didn't send His wrath, we sometimes erroneously conclude that what we couldn't have been too bad. That is a self-destructive assumption. The people in Athens were breaking the first four commandments. God winked at something for which He had at other times *killed* people! He winked at them when they were ignorant. But now...

Don't ever let a "but now..." catch you unaware. When you see a "but now" somewhere, it means that what went on before is now null and void. God was willing to wink because of the Greeks' ignorance, but the "but now" canceled two things: It canceled their ignorance, because now that they've heard the truth spoken by Paul, they know better; and it meant that the season of God's winking was over.

> GOD MAY WINK IN YOUR IGNORANCE, BUT IT IS NEVER HIS INTENTION TO LEAVE YOU IGNORANT ABOUT ANYTHING.

The apostle James said that *to him who knows to do good and doesn't, it is sin* (James 4:17). That doesn't imply that if you don't know what you're doing, it isn't sin; it means that when you know that what you're doing is not good and you do it anyway, then you are deliberately sinning before God. Paul called the men of Athens to repentance because what they did from that point on would be a deliberate violation of God's commands, and He would no longer wink at it.

God may wink in your ignorance, but it is never His intention to leave you ignorant about anything. He will see the exact point at which you become aware of your sin, and then He will call you to repentance. You may have gotten away with it for a long time. *But now...*

EYES THAT LOOK FOR ME

To say that God looks for us may lead us to make the mistake of assuming He doesn't know where we are. That would be true if God were human. However, the idea of God looking for us amplifies and magnifies His almost relentless desire to move in our lives. A more accurate interpretation of "for" would be to say that God is looking "for the benefit of," or "on behalf of," us. It is an expression of God's persistent yearning to exert influence on us and in us, in order to bring us closer to His divine will for us.

The following verse is a very graphic and picturesque illustration of God's searching on our behalf:

> *For the eyes of the LORD run to and fro throughout the whole earth, to show himself strong in the behalf of them whose heart is perfect toward him.* (2 Chronicles 16:9)

Both behavior and intent are obvious in the Scripture above. The eyes of a concerned, caring God are seeking. He's looking all over the world, to and fro, back and forth, up and down, leaving no stone unturned, no cave unexplored.

He's not just looking for something; He's looking for something to do on our behalf. God's goal of showing Himself strong for His people is the thing that drives Him to search. This is a portrait of God on a relentless search; and He's not going to stop until He finds what He's looking for. His eyes run "to and fro" as He searches for someone to show Himself strong for.

Now take a look at another picture of *to and fro*:

> *Surely every man walketh in a vain show: surely they are disquieted in vain: he heapeth up riches, and knoweth not who shall gather them.* (Psalm 39:6)

The *New International Version* says it like this: *"Man is a mere phantom as he goes to and fro: he bustles about, but only in vain; he heaps up wealth, not knowing who will get it."*

Let's look at the picture this paints. Man here is walking to and fro. Walking usually speaks of one's conduct and lifestyle. The writer of this psalm says that the man in this verse is one who is walking back and forth, to and fro, in a show of vanity. He is described as a *"phantom."* That word suggests that he is a shadow, a representation of the fragility of life. It's like saying man is nothing but a mist or vapor; no more than a shadow going to and fro in a vain show.

Imagine that our man is a traveler journeying through a desert. He's tired, he's weary, he's thirsty, he's hungry. Now comes the vain show. His eyes light up, because off in the horizon he sees a shimmering oasis. He picks up the pace and finally reaches the place he thought contained water in abundance. But where he expected to find cool water, he discovers hot sand. For all its shimmering in the distance, there was no payoff. It was a mirage, a vain show. And throughout his desert excursion, he continues seeking and not finding.

That is the image of a person who spends his whole life going after things that never fulfill him; who has spent time, energy, resources, emotions, and focus chasing things that don't satisfy the longing and the thirst of the soul. It is a life lived *to and fro* in a vain show. You may have seen lives like that. Many people live lives obsessed with nothingness. The things they invested much of their effort in have not proven worthy of being desired. These people are addicted to the chase and unimpressed with the catch. Their motives may be pure. They are looking for something they can delight in. They want fulfillment, refreshment, and rest. Some search for healing, others for deliverance. There is nothing wrong with any of that. The problem is, they're not finding any of that. They're looking to and fro and finding nothing important to grab and hold on to.

The bigger problem is that when they've been in the desert for a long time, they become weak and delirious. They get so desperate and thirsty that they'll take anything that looks like water, and be satisfied. That's the dangerous thing about a vain, desert life. You get weak, and when you get weak, you become prey for something or someone who has been waiting for you to get to this point.

Remember that God's eyes are looking to and fro, and man is walking to and fro. Now let's see who else is in this to and fro mix...

> *Now there was a day when the sons of God came to present themselves before the LORD, and Satan came also among them. And the LORD said unto Satan, Whence comest thou? Then Satan answered the LORD, and said, From going to and fro in the earth, and from walking up and down in it.*
>
> (Job 1:6–7)

There it is. On the earth and going to and fro is none other than that lying accuser of the brethren, satan himself. If satan is going to and fro, and we are going to and fro, sooner or later we're bound to run into each other. That is not somebody we want to meet in our travels (especially when we're weak), because of his intentions for anyone he meets on the road:

> *Be sober, be vigilant; because your adversary the devil, as a roaring lion, walketh about, seeking whom he may devour.*
>
> (1 Peter 5:8)

Man is going to and fro. Satan is also going to and fro. Man is looking for hope, deliverance, refreshment, fulfillment, intimacy, and delight. Satan is looking to devour, gulp down, and destroy man. His goal is not merely to wound you; his goal is to crush you. His goal is not just to give you a bad name or to take you down a peg or two. He wants to swallow you until there is no more of you left. And he's traveling around looking specifically for *you*.

The good news is that satan is so obsessed with us that he's not paying attention to the eyes of God. They've been following him in his to and fro, too, watching him watch us.

> **When God finds a person whose heart is right, He will attach Himself to that person.**

The Bible says God's eyes are searching for us for the purpose of showing Himself strong on our behalf. The phrase *"show himself strong"* (2 Chronicles 16:9) means "to attach to, to hold strongly to, to fasten to." God says that when He finds a person whose heart is right, whose eyes are on Him, and who is weak in the battle, He will attach Himself to that person, and He will attach Himself so closely that He becomes the very strength that person needs. A heart that is right is not necessarily a heart that is sinless; it is a heart that has acknowledged its helplessness against sin and its hope in deliverance from almighty God. God says He will meet that person in his weakness and become his strength.

Do you see the pattern? You are looking for fulfillment and intimacy and blessings. The enemy is looking for you. God is looking at both, ready to come to your aid the moment you get your eyes off of the blessings and put them on Him—it is then that He will become your strength, fight your battles, and bless you exceeding abundantly above all you could ask or think. And the enemy will see you rise victorious as God attaches Himself to you and becomes your strength.

When I'm too weak to do for myself, I have a God whose eyes are on me, waiting for the opportunity to be strong.

Now to that question I have grappled with for years—since September 11, 2001: *"Did You see that, God?"*

Yes, He saw it. He saw us when we were struck. He saw us fall. He saw every tear. He saw every man, woman, and child beneath the rubble. He saw us weak. And He will see us through every step of putting things right in His sight, for the eyes of God see and take into account...*everything.*

FOUR

YOUR LIPS TO GOD'S EARS

> "Had I but serv'd my God with half the zeal
> I serv'd my king, He would not in mine age
> Have left me naked to mine enemies."
> —William Shakespeare, Henry VIII

I'm not the best listener in the world. Sometimes there's so much going on in my mind that conversation is difficult to insert. It's like trying to stuff another folder into a filing cabinet that's already crammed full. To me, there's order to it, and information is easy to retrieve and add to. But it doesn't make sense to anyone else. It's like my study at home: To others it looks like a mess, but I know where everything is, and I know if anything has been moved.

The problem is not too much information coming into my ears each day; it's filing it all away. I'm running out of storage space in my brain! And I only focus on one or two or maybe half a dozen people at a time who want to talk to me. God has *billions* talking to Him, and He can give His undivided attention to all of them *at the same time*—all the time! I can barely order takeout on the phone while my wife gives me instructions about what side dishes to include.

To me, God's hearing is one of His most impressive features. Like His eyes, the ears of God are a lot less complicated in their operation than our ears are. Our ears are comprised of three major parts: the outer, middle, and inner ear. The outer ear acts as a receiver, the middle ear is sort of an amplifier, and the inner ear functions as a transmitter.

This inner ear transmitter sends information to the brain, where it is sorted as to what we heard, where it came from, how loud it was, what it related to, etc. God's ears simply hear, period. There's no elapsed time between something said and something heard. God not only hears it as we say it, but He also heard it *before* we spoke or even thought it!

> **THERE ARE NO NEWS FLASHES WITH GOD.**

God's ears reveal something to us about His omniscience: He hears all because He knows all, and He knows all because He hears all. There are no news flashes with God. There are no surprises with Him. You don't come up with an idea, then share it with God. He already heard the idea before you came up with it, because the hearing of God is *spiritual* in nature. He hears much more than what we merely say. He hears what we think, what we feel, what we want, what we meant to say, what our spirit says, and what's hidden in our heart.

God's hearing also reveals His omnipresence and His omnipotence. He hears in all places, at all times, at the same time. There is nothing He cannot hear. There is not a word uttered from the lips, in the mind, or in the heart of man that God does not hear. As awesome as all of that is, the thing I find most incredible about the ears of God is the fact that He uses them to *listen*. God is a great listener—and He doesn't have to be, because He knows everything we have said, are saying, and will say, and He has known it forever! But still He listens to us pray. Still He listens to our praise. Still He listens to us cry. He actively *listens* to us! He never thinks, *Oh no, not you again.* He never says, "Yeah, yeah, I know all that—tell Me something I don't know." He gives us His full and undivided attention, as if He is hearing it all fresh and new. It's an incredibly loving parent who takes the time to listen to what he already knows his children are about to say. But that's our God.

In order to really listen, we humans have to be interested, concerned, and ready to respond. We must also be attentive enough to catch all the nuances and inflections that might indicate a conflict in what's being said. God doesn't have to do any of that. He knows if you're lying or telling the truth. He knows if your heart is breaking and you're just trying to put up a good front. He knows *everything.* Yet, He still listens. He still encourages us to say what we want to say. He still wants to hear from us.

In the book of Titus we are warned about "idle talk." Idle talk is talk that is meaningless or worthless. It is talk that is not edifying. Titus says idle words *cry out to God.* Think about that: Idle words reach the listening ears of God. He hears what we say about somebody behind their back; and our careless words cry out to God on behalf of the people we hurt when we say them.

God Hears, God Cares

One of the most striking images of God's listening abilities is found in Psalm 102:

Hear my prayer, O LORD, and let my cry come unto thee.
Hide not thy face from me in the day when I am in trouble;
incline thine ear unto me: in the day when I call answer
me speedily....I watch, and am as a sparrow alone upon the
house top. (Psalm 102:1–2, 7)

Just before Psalm 102:1, right under the number of the psalm and before the first verse, there is an introduction that classifies the psalm. The Psalm 102 introduction identifies it as, *A Prayer of the afflicted, when he is overwhelmed, and poureth out his complaint before the LORD.* This particular psalm is one that is to be sung by a person who is afflicted and overwhelmed, and who goes to God about it. [2]

The ears of God are called upon by a specific kind of person. Notice how the Word of God identifies the person who prays the Psalm 102 prayer: Verse one says, *"Hear my prayer"*; while verse two asks God to *"incline Thine ear."* The Bible tells us three things about this person: he is afflicted, he is overwhelmed, and he has complaints. *"Afflicted"* is not as dramatic as it sounds. It is not the extreme idea of suffering from some debilitating illness—although it certainly can include that. The word *"afflicted"* used here is more like *sorrow*. This is a prayer or song for someone who is enduring grief. In today's vernacular, it is someone who is going through a "rough patch." Some people tend to be real cool when they walk with God. They're John Wayne—cool, calm, and in command. They have their act together. They don't hang out in the valleys; they leap from mountaintop to mountaintop. May the Lord continue to bless and keep those folks, but

---

[2] This song is part of a group of psalms called "penitential" psalms. These often had to do with repentance, like Psalm 51, for instance. This penitential song is not so much a confession of sin as it is a confession or an admittance of sorrow.

there are some people who know what it's like to go through a rough patch. I sure do!

Verse two of the psalm says the afflicted person *calls upon God in a day of trouble*. "Trouble," as we examined in a previous chapter, presents the picture of a person who is trapped or hemmed in. They're in a tight place. Their back is up against the wall. They don't know which way to turn, and even if they did, it wouldn't matter, because things are so tight that turning is impossible. Can't go forward, can't go backward, can't go sideways. Falling down even requires a move, and moving isn't an option.

It brings great sorrow when we're in a set of circumstances where we feel confined, confused, can't work our way out, can't think, pay, squeeze, or calculate our way out. Sometimes a tight place is the only thing holding us up! But it gets us on our spiritual knees, where we are ready to allow God to have a genuine effect upon us.

> GOD KNOWS EVERYTHING. YET, HE STILL WANTS TO HEAR FROM US.

The psalm also refers to a person who is *overwhelmed*. Not only are issues hemming them in, but they're also weighing them down. The word *"overwhelmed"* relates to clothing; it means *to be clothed in something*. This is a person whose struggles, problems, and decisions in life are like heavy pieces of clothing draped over them. Their experience has dressed them in a shroud of sorrow. Sorrow has an impact on how people see us. When we're clothed in something heavy, it affects our appearance. Our real shape and look are covered.

Sorrow doesn't always look bad. Sometimes it gets all dressed up and tries to appear free from strife. Have you ever seen a person who wants you to believe that all is well with them? If you observe them long enough, you perceive that something is weighing them down. You sense misery, depression, or sorrow upon them. Those things live deep in the heart, yet are worn like a garment.

If a person wears sorrow for too long, it becomes unbearable. Sooner or later they start to have complaints. The psalm of one who is entreating the listening ear of God is the psalm of one who *"poureth out his complaint before the* LORD*"* (Psalm 102:1). But complaints don't necessarily have to do with dissatisfaction. The word for "complaint" is an interesting one: It means *groans and moans*; specifically, ones that are *muffled*. That is not a person who is vocal about their struggle. They don't display a burst of outrage. Rather, this "complainer" is going through a valley, and deep down inside they are being squeezed from all sides. They can't cry out, because they're all cried out. Their pain may be simply too deep to express. They wish they had someone to talk to, but even if they did, they wouldn't know how to express it. The cloak of sorrow that covers them has become a muzzle, preventing them from expressing their pain. Their only option is to pour out their complaints before the Lord. They take their sorrow, their heaviness, their loneliness, and whatever else that weighs them down and pour them into the ear of God.

> ONE OF THE MOST INSULTING THINGS YOU CAN DO TO A PERSON IS TO IGNORE HIM.

Your Lips to God's Ears

When I was a little boy, every now and then I would get an ear infection and my mama would send me to the store to get some oil. She called it "sweet oil." She would warm up this oil and tell me to lean my head over to the side. Then she would pour the warm oil into my ear. As a little boy, I figured if the oil went in, it would eventually come out of my head somewhere—there were too many holes in my head for it not to. But it never did! In a little while, there'd be a *pop!*—and I could hear again. I learned later in a biology class that the oil had been absorbed into my body, and as that happened, a healing began.

The psalmist poured his sorrow into the ear of God, and his sorrow was absorbed into the very essence of the personhood of God. When we pour our pain into God's ear, He compassionately absorbs our sorrow, swings into action for us, and like a balm of warm oil, His healing begins.

God Listens to You

One of the most insulting things you can do to a person is to ignore them. I can't tell you how many couples I've counseled where the complaint has been that one of them doesn't listen to the other. Invariably, somewhere in the conversation, the wife will say to me, "He just doesn't listen." One time I asked a woman, "How does that make you feel when your husband doesn't listen?" She answered, "Insignificant."

My wife has said to me a few times, "Sweetheart, you are not listening to me." She was right; and I realized that I actually insulted her with my lack of consideration.

It is a betrayal of a relationship to refuse to listen. It is unkind not to honor another person with our listening, or to assume that we know what they are going to say before they say it. Some people, while someone is talking to them, will tune out and prepare a response, instead of listening. God knows what we're going to say, yet He honors us with His listening. That is an example of divine respect that we need to follow in our dealings with others.

Sometimes people only half listen, then try to fix whatever the problem is so they don't have to listen anymore. Men are good at that—especially with our wives and children, because our provider/protector response kicks in. If you tell me a problem, I figure it's my job to fix it. It's a reflex. Sometimes people don't need you fix things; they simply want you to listen to them.

> THE FACT THAT GOD HEARS ME WITHOUT CONDEMNING ME IS AN EXPRESSION OF HIS MERCY.

God cares enough to listen. When the psalmist said, *"Hear my prayer, O LORD,"* he was really saying, "Please pay attention to my prayer, God." Hearing this way means that we consider the interests of the person we are listening to and that we intend to respond to what we hear. It is giving our *undivided attention* to them. The listening attention of God is a function of both His grace and His mercy. It is a function of His grace because we do not deserve His attention in any way; it is a gift freely given. It is a function of His mercy because if God hears all, then He hears my sin, and the fact that He hears me without condemning me is an expression of His mercy—which endures forever!

I used to think that I had to prepare what I was going to say to God or He wouldn't listen to me. As a child, I thought some of my prayers didn't get answered because they weren't pretty enough. If we're not careful, our whole prayer life can get off track by listening to somebody else's prayers. When

I was young, I was amazed at some of the prayers people would pray at my church. We would start our church services with something we called "devotion." The "devoted brothers" would pray in a way that could tend to confuse a person about prayer. One fellow used to pray, "Lord, here we come, once more and again, knee bent and body bowed, facing mother dust! Lord, we thank You that the room we slept in last night was not the walls of our grave, the bed was not our cooling board, and the cover was not our winding."

I think what that meant was, *Lord, I'm sure glad I ain't dead this mornin'!*

Some people go to God scraping and apologizing. "I don't mean to bother You, Lord..." God is a God who *desires* to hear from you! He loves you—you're not a pest to Him. There are some three hundred million people in this country, and every one of us could pray at the same time in countless languages, dialects, and accents, and God wouldn't miss a single prayer! He wouldn't send your blessing over to somebody else by mistake. He wouldn't forget where you are, where you've been, or where you've come from. He's a God who hears *you*. He loves you right where you are, and He wants to hear from you just the way you are, saying just what you have to say. We don't have to force God to hear from us, and we don't have to excuse ourselves to Him when we pray.

The suffering psalmist in Psalm 102 asked God to *"Incline thine ear."* In fact, so there would be no confusion, he said, *"Incline thine ear to me."* In other words, "Lord, lean this way and listen in my direction." What a wonderful picture: Not only does God listen, He also *leans down* to listen to us! He gets up close and personal. That's amazing. We can't count high enough to number the things God has to think about, do, feel, say, exert influence over, or control in one second of time all over the world. Yet, at every moment of our lives, He's available and He is bent in our direction to listen to us and to give us His personal, undivided attention.

The psalmist also said that God will do this *"in his day of trouble."* The word *"day"* is not a reference to a twenty-four-hour period of time. It has to do with a specific period of one's experience. It is a particular season or defined series of moments. This is significant because it points to the fact that the individual who seeks the ear of God is experiencing a specific set of circumstances that require the ear of God. There's a crisis going on, and the person needs God's ears attuned to it.

God's attention, His efforts, and His presence are not to be taken lightly. We have to be careful not to be loose in using His name, not to let slip a meaningless *Oh my God!* There is *power* attached to the name of God! If you don't mean it, don't say it. Respect the name of God. But when you do need Him, don't hesitate to call Him as many times as you think is necessary. He'll hear you, listen to you, and lean in to give you His focused attention.

The author of Psalm 102 understood that. In his day of trouble, he called on the Lord. He let God know that this was a serious situation. "Lord," he cried, "this is a particularly bad time for me. The weight of my sorrow, distress, and discouragement is suffocating me. It's overwhelming me. Please, God, I need Your attention, and I need it *speedily.*"

GOD HEARS OUT OF TIME

In the day when I call, answer me speedily.

(Psalm 102:2)

Sometimes we need to hear from God, but we don't have the time to wait. We pray something like, "Lord, I need Your help—*now*. I don't mean any disrespect, but I don't have time for any 'knee bent and body bowed.' I need to hear a word from You. I'm cutting to the chase: *Help!* Amen." That sure has been my prayer at times—*Help! Amen.* Has that ever been your prayer? Have you ever gone to God with a rush order? One translation of Psalm 102:2 says, *"Answer me quickly."* In other words, "Please hurry!"

One time while I was on the road, I ordered some clothes. The man told me, "We can ship it to you regular freight or as a rush order, overnight." The writer of this psalm asked God for a rush-order blessing. It used to sound almost arrogant to me for people to go to God and say, "Look, I need Your answer right away on this! Put a rush on it, will You?!"

> GOD LOVES YOU RIGHT WHERE YOU ARE, AND HE WANTS TO HEAR FROM YOU JUST THE WAY YOU ARE.

Then I thought about it...and I realized that it's not only a permissible prayer, it's a reasonable one. It points out the immediacy of God's hearing. I call *on* Him in the earthly realm, but I call *to* Him in the spiritual realm—for that's where He dwells. I've called *on* Him "in my day of trouble," which means I call Him at a specific period of time. But God doesn't dwell in time, He dwells in *eternity*. So, from my tight place in time, I call out to Him in eternity. I have taken my request, wrapped it in my prayer, and sent it from Earth's time-bound realm out to timeless eternity and into the very ear of God. When God hears my prayer, frequently He responds in a twinkling of an eye, because He doesn't have to think about the answer. He knew the answer before I even asked the question. He heard my thoughts before I thought to pray. Sooner than right now and quicker than not yet, God sends the answer out of eternity and and provides an answer to the prayer, because in Him there is no delay, no tomorrow, no later on. He lives in a state of perpetual "now."

However, we humans don't live in that dimension; we live in a dimension of time, which means that a process must take place before we can receive our answer from God. While the journey of a prayer from the earthly realm to the spiritual realm takes no time, the trip going in the other direction is a *process*. God doesn't have to process our petitions and prayers; but since we humans are not perfect, His answer enters a human-bound process, which can often delay His answer. It can take a second, or it can take a century. It all depends on our readiness to believe and receive, and upon what is occurring in the spiritual realm around us.

The story of Elijah, in 1 Kings 18:22–46, illustrates this principle well. The prophet went up to Mount Carmel for a duel with the 450 prophets of the idol god baal. This was not a fair fight. With God on his side, Elijah had them greatly outnumbered. The goal was to see whose god was the *real* God: Elijah's God, or baal. Elijah said, "The God who answers by fire, He is God."

Scripture says the 450 prophets called on baal...and nothing happened.

After awhile, Elijah started to make fun of them. He said, "Well, fellas, maybe you're not calling loudly enough. Maybe your god has a hearing problem. Why don't you holler a little louder?" Elijah had set them up because he knew that baal was a god made by men. He had ears, but he couldn't hear them, no matter how long or loudly they called out. "Maybe he is deep in thought, or busy, or traveling," Elijah taunted them. "Maybe he is sleeping and must be awakened."

The Bible says these guys started cutting themselves and calling out as loudly as they could.

Finally, around evening, Elijah said, "Look, I've got to be getting home, and you boys have wasted too much of my time. Now it's my turn." First, Elijah repaired the altar. Then, knowing that he was expecting fire, he completely saturated the altar with water, because he didn't want any of those baal folks claiming that something spontaneously combusted on the altar. He wanted no mistake with where the fire came from. He soaked everything in water, including the wood. Then he prayed and called upon the Lord...and fire fell on the altar and fried everything! But before Elijah opened his mouth, the fire was already on the way. God heard the petition before the challenge came out of Elijah's mouth. However, they still had to wait until they prepared the altar to receive the fire that had already been sent from eternity.

> THE ONLY DELAY IN ANSWER TO OUR PRAYERS IS THAT GOD HAS OUR BLESSING; WE JUST CAN'T HANDLE IT YET.

When we call upon the name of the living God, He hears our prayer and answers it. The only delay is that He has to prepare us for the answer. He has our blessing; we just can't handle it yet.

Sometimes, however, the delay is caused by factors beyond our control. There was once a man named Daniel, who fasted and prayed to God for three weeks before he finally got a knock on the door. Standing there was an angelic messenger with the answer to his prayer. Though Daniel was frightened at the sudden appearance of the angel, he must have been thinking, *What happened?—What took you so long to get here?* Daniel could ask a question like that because he knew he was in right relationship with God. He knew that there was nothing he was doing that would prevent God from answering him speedily. He was just curious to know what the holdup was. The messenger answered, "God heard your prayer twenty-one days ago, but as I was on my way to you with the answer, the prince of Persia blocked my way" (Daniel 10:12).

The prince of Persia was a territorial demon who was assigned to that area to keep out the blessings and the messengers of God. The devil doesn't want us to be blessed, doesn't want us to be healed, doesn't want us to overcome, doesn't want us delivered, happy, drug-free, prosperous, or promoted. The messenger said he'd been on the way with the answer for twenty-one days because God had heard Daniel's prayer the first day he prayed it. There were delays in getting the answer to Daniel. But God foresees delays, and while it may not appear to be so to human eyes, the arrival of His answer is always in perfect timing for the person and their circumstance.

Your blessing or your answer from God is on the way. What the demons don't know is that they can't stop God from answering you: He answers as soon as you pray. The demons don't get into the process until it's too late to do anything about it. They're wasting their time, but they're too arrogant and hardheaded to realize it. All they can do is hold things up. But the more things they hold up, the more prayers you send up. The more prayers you send up, the more answers get built up. And eventually all those answers from God push their way through every attempt to delay or deflect them.

God saw Daniel fasting and praying for twenty-one days before Michael the Archangel was finally dispatched to push his way through. In the book of Revelation, it is Michael and his crew who take on the serpent and his boys and kick them out of heaven. God didn't send Hank or Bernice or Herbert or any of the regular angels. He sent the general!

Every time somebody gossiped about your situation, God heard it and sent comfort, even before you got around to praying for it. Psalm 56:8 says, *"God saved your tears."* That means He heard your cries before you asked Him to dry your tears. God has been sending answers to prayers your mother prayed over you as a child. Sometimes you don't need a blessing, you just need to hold on until your answer arrives.

> PRAISE GOD RIGHT NOW FOR THE ANSWERS THAT ARE ON THE WAY!

Do you want to know how to make God's ears perk up? Praise Him right now for the answers that are on the way. Anybody can shout about what's going on now, but I dare you to praise God about the things He's *going* to do. Walk by faith and not by sight, for it is *faith* that pleases God! Our biggest shout should not come from what we see. We have to get to the place where we rejoice about what we know but can't see. Shout when you sign up for that first college course—don't wait for graduation! Praise Him for your promotion on the first day of your new job! God is listening!

I once had a suitcase in my study that I hadn't unpacked for months. Every time I looked at it, I started praising God. I had packed that bag while we were in our old house because I knew God was going to bless us with a new home. I packed it after being turned down nine times for a loan. The answer was delayed because it had to work its way through people who didn't like what I did for a living, people who didn't like what color I was, people who just didn't like me. But God told me to keep on seeking, keep on asking, and keep on knocking, because the answer was on the way.

For a long time, I looked at that suitcase sitting in the corner of my new study in my new home. To other people, it looked like clutter and procrastination. But I knew better. To me it was a constant reminder: *God listens to me!*

It has been a few years since that season of my life. I did finally unpack the bag. I had to—there was no room in my new study for it. When I think about that, I'm grateful that God doesn't have any storage problems when it comes to listening to me...and I shout all over again, *"Hallelujah!"* Our awesome God listens to us!

FIVE

THE NOSE OF GOD: BEYOND APPEARANCE

"The conversion of a soul is the miracle of a moment,
but the making of a saint is the task of a lifetime."
—Alan Redpath, *The Making of a Man of God*

As I approached my study on *the nose of God*, I must admit I was apprehensive. To spend time examining somebody's nose seems almost rude—especially if the nose belongs to God. Anytime we deal with the things of God, we're treading on holy ground.

A nose doesn't seem like much at first; just a piece of flesh in the middle of your face—*BAM!*—a nose, smack-dab in the center of the most exposed part of your body. If you were looking at your nose in the mirror right now, it would have just gotten a little bigger. Try an experiment: Have a conversation with someone, but don't look them in the eyes, look at their nose. See how long it takes for the person to ask, "Hey, what are you looking at my nose for?" In staring at someone's nose, you've crossed personal space boundaries, which tends to make people feel uncomfortable.

A nose can make or break your whole look. If a woman has a face like an angel and a nose like Jimmy Durante, some folks aren't able to get past that. Now, before you're tempted to start feverishly flipping through your Bible for Scripture references about God not looking at the outward appearance, let me save you the trouble: It's 1 Samuel 16:7, just a few verses before the prophet anoints a little teenage shepherd boy named David to be the next king of Israel. David is described as *"ruddy, and withal of a beautiful countenance, and goodly to look to"* (1 Samuel 16:12). In other words, David's nose was probably not a distraction.

Truth is, a nose can challenge the appearance of a person if it is deformed or misshapen. If it appears too big or too small or too crooked, it throws people off. People who don't like their own noses will tell you that the worst thing about having an ugly nose is that you can't hide it. It wouldn't be so bad if your nose weren't so "out there." That may seem ridiculous to you if there is nothing wrong with your nose. But a person who has had to deal with people's response to their nose is not laughing with you.

There used to be a television situation comedy called *The Brady Bunch,* about an extended family of three sons and three daughters. In one of the episodes, the eldest girl, Marsha, gets hit in the face with a football and her nose gets all bruised and swollen. Up to that point, Marsha was used to getting pretty much any boy in school to go out with her. In fact, her sister Jan had an issue with that. Jan wasn't ugly or anything; she just wasn't Marsha—who was the one everybody favored.

In this episode, Marsha has a date with the captain of the football team. However, those plans change abruptly when he sees Marsha's nose. He makes up a lame excuse and backs out of the date because he doesn't want to mess up his image by being seen in public with Marsha and her queen-size schnozzola.

By now you may be wondering, *What do Jimmy Durante, Marsha Brady, and David have to do with the nose of God?* Simple: A nose is a very obvious and prominent feature, but it's not an important *feature*—it's an important *organ.* That is, as an operating part of our anatomy, its use by (and usefulness to) the body is substantial. Most people treat the nose as little more than a facial accessory. When you describe it, you don't say, "His nose really sucks in a lot of air." You describe it by its appearance, therefore ascribing it worth according to how pleasing it is to the eye. However, its *function* is what matters, for it plays an important role in the overall biological, physiological, and anatomical systems of our bodies.

God endures our warped perceptions when it comes to His "nose." Like ours, His is a nose that breathes and smells. Breathing and smelling

> **MOST PEOPLE FAIL TO GET BEYOND THE PHYSICAL COSMETICS OF SALVATION AND WORSHIP.**

may seem like the dullest and most mundane of pursuits. Yet, within those ordinary activities, the nose of God is distinct from all other parts of His anatomy, for it contains the extraordinary revelation of salvation and worship. Our relationship with God, His undying love for us, and our expressions of adoration and appreciation to Him are reflected in the construction and performance of the nose. Yet, the majority of people fail to get beyond the physical cosmetics of salvation and worship. We see them as accessories in our walk with God, rather than essentials, and our efforts go into "beautifying" them before the world rather than "becoming" them before God.

God is seeking people who will worship Him in spirit and in truth. He is seeking *worshippers*. Instead, He's finding pseudo-spiritual minstrels who puff out imaginary glory while working themselves up into an emotional, ego-induced fervor. He's seeking worshippers; He's finding singers and shouters. God desires people who want to find Him; but too many people are overly concerned with how divine our holy dance looks. Worship is deeper and more important than that. We should worship, yes; but we need to know *why* people worship, and learn *how* to worship. If we stop at the surface of worship, we've missed the point.

THE BREATH OF GOD

The nose is the natural pathway by which air enters the body in the normal course of breathing. A number of correlating images can be seen in Scripture: In Genesis, God is seen breathing the breath of life into the nostrils of man. Man is distinct from animals in that while all living creatures have life in them, only man has *God's* breath of life in him:

> *And the* LORD *God formed man of the dust of the ground, and breathed into his nostrils the breath of life; and man became a living soul.* (Genesis 2:7)

The Scripture says God *"breathed"* His *"breath"* into man's nostrils. The Hebrew word for *"breathed"* means to *inflate, puff, kindle,* or *ignite*. On the other hand, it also means *to snuff out*. In 2 Samuel 22:9 and Job 41:20, the Bible speaks of the nostrils of God venting His holy anger against wickedness and the destruction that follows.

The word *"breath"* has a slightly different spin on it. The translation for this Hebrew word is "a puff" or "a wind."

However, it also means "inspiration," "soul," and "spirit." More specifically, it refers to *the Spirit of God*. In other words, God breathed His Spirit into man. If man was created in the image of God, and God is a Spirit, then He breathed Himself—His *Spirit*—into man.

The nose doesn't actually cause us to breathe. Biologically and anatomically, we breathe *through* the nose, not *with* it. Many people assume that the nose is the organ with which the body breathes or that breathing begins in the lungs. Neither the nose nor the lungs are responsible for breathing. The reason we breathe is so that our bodies can do what they were designed to do: To live. In order to do that, our cells (the basic units of life in our bodies) need oxygen. That oxygen is carried by the blood, which is pumped throughout the body by the heart. A living body burns up oxygen; so the cells continually put pressure on the heart to send more oxygen through the blood. The heart puts pressure on the lungs to inflate. And that is what makes us breathe. To put it succinctly: The need of the cells to live causes us to breathe. The blood and the heart are called into service by the need of the millions of cells that make up the human body. That's why we breathe.

And that's why God breathes, also. He gave us life by breathing His breath into us. When sin entered the world, we became separated from Him, and we started dying. Like the cells in our bodies, we need His breath—His "oxygen"—to live. That need puts pressure on the heart of God, and He responds by sending His Spirit, His "wind," His breath, His oxygen, through the blood of His Son Jesus.

Did you know that the oxygen in your body can get to your cells only by your blood? Even though the cells of your

93

skin are exposed to the oxygen in the air, they can't absorb it. It can come to them only through the blood. Likewise, in our spiritual lives, we have access to the "oxygen" of God only because of the blood of Jesus.

We inhale oxygen. We exhale carbon dioxide. If we were to breathe only carbon dioxide, eventually we would die. Carbon dioxide is what's left when a cell uses up its oxygen by living. Carbon dioxide leaves the body the same way the oxygen came in, through the blood. That same blood that brought us life-giving oxygen is the same blood that removes the carbon dioxide that would poison us and kill us if it were allowed to stay in our bodies. And the same blood that was shed for us on the cross washes us clean and takes away the poison of sin in our life.

Every once in awhile, I make my way to the gym to get in a little workout. It doesn't take long before I start breathing a little harder and a little deeper. That's because something is happening to the cells of my body. They are using up oxygen faster than normal. That means carbon dioxide is being produced at a faster rate. Higher than normal levels of carbon dioxide in our body automatically triggers increased breathing.

WE WERE NOT CREATED THE WAY WE WERE BY ACCIDENT.

In other words, the heart is trying to get more oxygen to the cells, which is why we breathe harder. The parallel between that and the breathing of God is that increased oxygen use through exercise means more regular and efficient elimination of carbon dioxide. If we liken oxygen to the Spirit of God and carbon dioxide to sin, then when we exercise ourselves unto godliness according to Paul's exhortation in 1 Timothy 4:8, we incorporate more of the Holy Spirit into our living, and the sin that effort brings to the surface can be more efficiently carried away by the blood.

We were not created the way we were by accident. God did not just grab a handful of dust off the ground, mix it with a little spit, mold us into a form, and call us *man*. God is a God of all wisdom. He doesn't waste anything, and He certainly didn't waste a thing when He made us. God made our bodies to reflect His glory. God is love, which means His glory is seen in His love. The apostle John tells us how God loves us:

> *God showed how much he loved us by sending his only Son into the world so that we might have eternal life through him. This is real love. It is not that we loved God, but that he loved us and sent his Son as a sacrifice to take away our sins.* (1 John 4:9–10)

Did you know that the very biological makeup of your body carries the story of salvation? Your body is more than just a miracle of science. It is a miracle of Elohim. It is a miracle of I AM (Exodus 3:14). You are a miracle of the King of Glory, the Lord of Hosts, the Creator of all things. God has personally designed and crafted everything on you and in you. No artist presents a work that he has not signed; similarly, God has deposited into your DNA His signature, which is the story of His love for you—the story of your salvation. You were a miracle to God before your father and mother ever even met.

A WONDER OF GOD

When you look at yourself in the mirror, know that *"fearfully and wonderfully made"* (Psalm 139:14) are not just words that a psalmist tossed in a song. That phrase literally means that when God made you—when He knitted your arms and legs together in your mother's womb—He looked at you and said, "Mmm, mmm, mmm, what a wonder!" That is what you are to God: A *wonder!*

Keep in mind that there is no time between God's getting an idea and His making the idea reality. In fact, in the unfathomable depths of His will, God wants something, decides to make it, then makes it and is pleased with it—all at the same time; and He does it just by speaking. God's thought instantly creates. If you really think about that, it'll make you shout. God said your name, fell in love with you, made you, and declared you "wonderful"—all in the same instant! It doesn't matter what anybody else told you about yourself, God says you're a wonder. And He put the biology in you to back it up.

> WHEN WAS THE LAST TIME YOU THANKED GOD FOR BREATHING LIFE INTO YOU?

Our physical body reflects the miracle of salvation. That's why we shouldn't treat our body like it doesn't matter. The body was designed to live and purposed to glorify and honor God. Every breath we take should remind us that we live only because God loves us; and because He loves us, He saved us; and because He saved us, we ought to live for Him.

When was the last time you thanked God for breathing life into you? When was the last time you gave Him credit for that?

The nose of God speaks to the choice that God made to give us life and sustain it. You can't talk about a nose without talking about breath, life, and blood, anymore than you can talk about the nose of God without mentioning Jesus, the Holy Spirit, and salvation.

THE FLIP SIDE

The nose not only allows air into the body, but it also protects the body by controlling the content of the air that comes in. Dust and particles, for example, come into the nose and then get trapped by little hairs in the nose called *cilia*. When we blow our nose, that action eliminates those particles from the body before they've had a chance to do any damage. God figuratively "blowing His nose" is His protecting and delivering His people from danger at the hand of their enemies.

> *By the blast of your nostrils the waters piled up. The surging waters stood firm like a wall; the deep waters congealed in the heart of the sea.* (Exodus 15:8 NIV)

In the passage above, God parted the Red Sea with "a *blast*" of His nostrils so Israel could walk through on dry land. Then, in verse ten, the same nose blew the water back down and drowned the Egyptians.

Psalm 18 is a song written by David when the Lord delivered him from his enemies—Saul in particular. David said that the blast of God's nostrils was a rebuke, or a scolding, to his enemies.

> *The valleys of the sea were exposed and the foundations of the earth laid bare at your rebuke, O LORD, at the blast of breath from your nostrils.* (Psalm 18:15 NIV)

Neshamah, the Hebrew word for "blast," contains dramatic imagery: that of a stallion snorting.

Anger is often typified by heavy breathing, especially through the nose. In Proverbs 22:24 we are cautioned not to make friendship with an *"angry"* man. The word for *"angry"* literally means "breathing place"; it's the same word used for "nose." Have you ever seen somebody who is really mad? Their nostrils start to flare and their breathing quickens.

The breath of God's nostrils is nothing to take lightly. When He's mad, He's not just standing around snorting and ranting while the angels avert their eyes, zip their lips, and cut a wide path around Him until He cools down. God's anger and breathing are always intentional and directed. If He's mad at you, He's coming to get you—and you can forget about running or hiding from a God who sees and knows everything.

Keep in mind that breathing is a function of the need of the cells in our bodies, not an action or choice initiated by the nose. When God gets angry, He always has a reason, and the reason always has to do with the needs of His people. Wrath is ignited in the nostrils of God when His people are oppressed or persecuted by their enemies. He then moves, because they need deliverance.

There is a flip side to the nose of God as it relates to the anger of God. In Isaiah 65, God is responding to Israel's prayer for deliverance from their enemies. In chapter 64, the people want God to show up and defend them the way He had in the past. They even got dramatic with it. They said, "Oh, that You would rend the heavens! That You would come down, that the mountains would shake at Your presence! Come on, Lord! Bring fire when You come—hot enough to make water boil and make Your name known to Your adversaries that they might tremble!" In other words, "Lord, we want You to put some fire in Your pocket and come on down here and put on a show so our enemies will be shaking in their sandals. You know, like You used to do. C'mon!"

I love Israel, because Israel would try to get God to move by calling Him on what He promised, as if they could catch Him slacking. They didn't come right out and say it, but they implied that God wasn't treating them (His *chosen* people, no less) any differently than He was treating the heathens. "Well, we thought *You* said *something* about us being *Your* people! We remember something about 'never leaving us or forsaking us.' Well, we're feeling mighty lonely down here, Lord. We're not saying we're forsaken per se, but You have been a little absent up in here."

> **When God gets angry, He always has a reason, and it always has to do with the needs of His people.**

But we can't be too hard on Israel, because we do the very same thing. "God, You said You would open up the windows of heaven if I bring You my tithe. Now, I'm not saying You lied, and I haven't checked the weather channel, but so far—I'm not saying it won't happen—but so far I haven't seen any blessings raining down from heaven. Oh, and by the way, *Father*, I do recall that You said something about giving me 'whatsoever I ask.' Maybe my mate got held up in the mail. I know You have the tracking numbers from my prayers—all six hundred of them—could You check on that for me? Appreciate it."

What Israel and a few of us fail to remember is that God's goal is to make us *holy*, not necessarily happy. Israel was praying for God to honor His relationship with them, and all the while they were still practicing idolatry, breaking His ordinances and commandments, and being self-righteous and prideful. They were looking to be delivered from their enemies, when they needed to be delivered from their sins.

I love how God responds to them. They want God to come out of heaven and vent His anger. They're looking for Him to work up a few good blasts from His nostrils and let fly in the direction of their enemies. But instead, look what God says:

> *I am sought of them that asked not for me; I am found of them that sought me not: I said, Behold me, behold me, unto a nation that was not called by my name. I have spread out my hands all the day unto a rebellious people, which walketh in a way that was not good, after their own thoughts; a people that provoketh me to anger continually to my face; that sacrificeth in gardens, and burneth incense upon altars of brick; which remain among the graves, and lodge in the monuments, which eat swine's flesh, and broth of abominable things is in their vessels; which say, Stand by thyself, come not near to me: for I am holier than thou. These are a smoke in my nose, and a fire that burneth all the day.*
>
> (Isaiah 65:1–5 KJV)

God's charge against Israel was that they had gone through the motions of being His people, but it was all superficial. That's what He meant when He told them that they *sought* Him but *"asked not"* for Him.

To *seek* means "to research or inquire after." It is a word that implies *worship*. Asking in this context means "to beg, entreat, or borrow." In other words, Israel was "playing church." They were coming into the building, doing all the posturing and pretending they needed to do to *look* holy, but they weren't seeking an audience with the *heart* of God. They weren't asking Him to meet their needs, change their lives, or honor them with His presence; they were just out to use His power for their means.

They liked being called God's chosen people, but they didn't want to live as if God had personally chosen them. They were bold about it, too! God said they were provoking Him to anger continually to His face. He gave them a laundry list of their offenses and told them that everything they'd been doing had been *"a smoke in My nose, a fire that burneth all the day."*

Israel was in rebellion. They had broken the law, and God said their relationship with Him was superficial and without substance. Israel had just asked God to come down out of heaven and show Himself to their enemies. That sounds like they had faith in God, but God said they didn't. Why didn't they? Because faith that is *seen* is not faith!

> *Faith is the substance of things hoped for, the evidence of things not seen.* (Hebrews 11:1)

The Israelites were asking God to do what He had already done *so they could look like chosen people to their enemies!* Their concern was with the *cosmetics* of being God's people, not with the *character* of being like Him. They were asking God to put on a show so they could look good.

A STENCH OF PRIDE

Have you ever looked at your circumstances and asked God to deliver you from them because you were ashamed of how bad you were looking to other people? Are you asking God for a spouse because you are embarrassed about your singleness? Why are you praying about your weight? Are you asking God for a car because you're ashamed of riding the bus? Have you ever wondered if you look "saved" enough to people? That is a stench in the nostrils of almighty God.

God will allow difficult situations into our lives to build character in us, but many people don't want the character. They just want the appearances. They want to look like some Scriptures, but not all of them. They'll wear a *God's Property* T-shirt, but how many will go out and, cash in hand, buy a T-shirt that says, *I know Him in the fellowship of His sufferings*, or *Obedience is better than sacrifice*, or *Though He slay me, yet will I trust Him.* You don't see those, because belief like that is not worn on the skin, it's worn on the heart.

> GOD IS NOT ABOVE SNORTING BLASTS OF ANGER AT US WHEN WE ENGAGE IN REBELLION, PRIDE, OR HYPOCRISY.

A superficial relationship with God is a smoke in His nose that burns all day long. What a graphic picture. Our hypocrisy causes a continual irritation in the nostrils of God! It's like there is something in His nose that He can't get out, and it's ticking Him off. God is saying that superficial relationships irritate Him. They get on His nerves.

If you've ever gotten too close to the barbecue pit and breathed some of the sooty smoke through your nose, you understand what God is saying. The smoke of hypocrisy going into His nose has aggravated and irritated the insides of His nostrils.

Where did that smoke come from? The prayers of the Israelites. Revelation 5:8 says the prayers of God's people are offered up to God as incense. The altar of incense in the Old

Testament tabernacle was the place where the morning and evening prayers were offered along with sacrifices. Incense is burned for its fragrance. Our prayers are incense before the Lord. Those that are accepted by Him are called a "sweet savor" in His nostrils. The Lord's words to Israel in Isaiah 65 were a response to the prayers they sent up in Isaiah 64. But, whereas the incense of prayers that are acceptable to God is a sweet aroma, the present smoke of Israel's supplications was a burning in His nostrils.

What do you do when there is something in your nose that is annoying and frustrating you? You blow your nose. And that's what God did. He got angry and vented His anger at Israel, telling them all He planned to do to them because of their rebellion.

God is not above snorting blasts of anger at us when we engage in unrepentant rebellion, pride, or hypocrisy. Jesus didn't die on that cross so we could work out our salvation on a part-time basis. Paul told us to exercise ourselves unto godliness. That means we have to make a choice to sweat a little and put some effort into becoming the people that God calls us to be.

Some of us eat the Word in awesome, Spirit-filled, Bible-believing churches. We pile our plates high every Sunday and throw in a little Bible study and conference hopping on the side. We become pew potatoes. We've gotten fat and happy, but not holy. God says we think we're "holier than thou," but that's far from the truth. We make His nose burn!

You will recognize it when God blows His nose. He will allow things to come into your life that will make you act on all those Bible verses you've been naming and claiming. He'll make you sweat. He'll allow you to go through some stuff that uses up everything you know about Him but didn't act on. He'll humble you. He'll put you in a tight place. And when you finally come to your senses and offer up your broken spirit and contrite heart instead of the fake and phony fluff that only impresses people in the front row, He'll be there to breathe Himself into you.

God loves you too much to let you continue on a path of mediocrity. We serve an excellent God, and He will not stop until all the excellence He put into us is worked out in us. The nose of God should make us remember that, because we are His children, He loves us enough to chasten us.

THE CONNECTION

The nose is connected to the middle ear via a structure called the Eustachian tube. The Eustachian tube equalizes air pressure on both sides of the eardrum. That's why, in an airplane, a change in cabin pressure will cause your ears to stop up. There's actually nothing in your ear but air, and "popping" your ears is just the act of relieving pressure. The pressure that is put on the eardrum can make it difficult to hear. However, it's not just a change in pressure from the outside that can have this effect on your ears. You can change the air pressure in the Eustachian tube by blowing your nose too hard or by having an illness or infection that blocks your nasal passages.

There is a cycle that occurs in this scenario with Israel in Isaiah 65 that illuminates our understanding of "the nose of God." God called Israel's prayers a continual burning in His nose. The same thing that occurs in our noses also occurred with God regarding Israel; and if we're not spiritually alert, it could happen to us. Continual, habitual sin pollutes the nasal passages of God and negatively impacts His hearing of our prayers.

When God is said to "hear" prayers, it means He has decided to accept them and answer them, as the Scriptures below reveal:

> *If my people, which are called by my name, shall humble themselves, and pray, and seek my face, and turn from their wicked ways; then will I hear from heaven, and will forgive their sin, and will heal their land.* (2 Chronicles 7:14)

> *I cried unto him with my mouth, and he was extolled with my tongue. If I regard iniquity in my heart, the Lord will not hear me: but verily God hath heard me; he hath attended to the voice of my prayer. Blessed be God, which hath not turned away my prayer.* (Psalm 66:17–20)

> *Likewise, ye husbands, dwell with them according to knowledge, giving honour unto the wife, as unto the weaker vessel, and as being heirs together of the grace of life; that your prayers be not hindered.* (1 Peter 3:7)

A SWEET SAVOR

> *I beseech you therefore, brethren, by the mercies of God, that ye present your bodies a living sacrifice, holy, acceptable unto God, which is your reasonable service.* (Romans 12:1)

You can become, thanks to Jesus, the sweet savor of sacrifice that is pleasing in the nostrils of God. The same nose that breathed life into you now breathes in the wonderful fragrance of the offering of yourself to Him.

Our nose is a prominent and obvious feature on our face. It helps define our whole look. But if you get caught up in the way your nose looks, you'll miss its real beauty: its purpose and function. The nose is connected to all the other sensory organs in the face—the ears, eyes, and mouth. It is designed to protect those organs and the rest of the body by filtering and carrying out dust and other debris. It has direct connections to the centers in the brain that affect mood, emotion, and memory. We can smell something, and it can instantly bring back wonderful memories, change our mood, and evoke vivid, passionate emotions.

When you look at the nose of God and see the visible manifestations of His love for you, like His provision and protection, remember that it's just a small thing compared to the real beauty of your salvation and your worship. Remember how all of God's senses are called into service on your behalf. Know that His protection includes filtering out the debris of sin from your life.

Most important, when you look at the nose of God, know that your sincere, holy, reasonable worship, made possible by your salvation, is inhaled by God and evokes within Him passionate and powerful emotions and feelings...about *you*.

Ask God to tell you what He thinks of you sometime. Every once in awhile, He'll speak into your spirit and hear Him say, *"Mmm, mmm, mmm. What a wonder you are!"*

Six

FROM THE MOUTH OF GOD: A WORD FROM THE WISE

"If words are to enter people's hearts and bear fruit,
they must be the right words shaped so as to pass
men's defenses and explode silently and effectually
within their minds."
—J. B. Phillips, *Making Men Whole*

he mouth of God is the most complete reflection of His overall personality. It's also the most engaging of all of His features. But does God really have to *speak*? What would He ever say that He doesn't already know? He is never "lonely," because He's God—He always has Himself, and He is more than enough. Yet, He does open His mouth...and life results, because that's what springs forth from Life Himself.

The depictions of God's voice in movies and on television shows is amusing. He is usually represented by a booming, bass-infused voice of authority, accompanied by the requisite thunder, lightning, and quaking earth. No wonder people are leery of getting to know God! Not that those images are completely off base: If anyone deserves mighty whirlwinds and falling mountains as punctuation for His discourse, it would be God. But it is deceiving to portray His dialogue with us as violent, dramatic outbursts or ominous threats of impending wrath. There is more to the mouth of God than that—there is far more *in* His mouth than that.

The mouth of God reveals His intentions and priorities. We've all seen or heard of encounters between fathers and the young men who desire to date their daughters. Dad is stern as he asks, "Son, what are your intentions toward my daughter?" He wants to know, up front, today, what this boy's plans are for his cherished little girl. When I was a young man, I didn't understand that question. "My *intentions*, sir? I *intend* to go to the movies with her and maybe grab a burger and fries later. Sir."

What I learned after having two daughters of my own, is that the question is designed to establish a covenant of trust between the father and the young man. The father wants it understood that you are about to walk out the door with someone who is of tremendous value to him. You warn the young man that you expect him to return your daughter to you in the same or better condition. Then you give him a serious look and ask menacingly, "Young man, what are your intentions?" If you've done your job right, the boy will be too afraid not to tell you the truth.

God made you a steward over your own life. Then one day He asked you to give it to Him. Your first question to God may have been, "What are Your intentions for me?" You are of great value to yourself. Some of us know what it's like to be abused and broken, and we're not in a hurry to hand ourselves over again just because someone asks us to. So we want to know, *God, what are Your intentions?* Unlike the young man and the dad, God doesn't have to be (nor could He ever be) intimidated into telling us the truth—He *is* Truth. He also understands our concern for our "treasure in earthen vessels." So, in order to ease our minds, God has told us—from His *mouth*—all of His intentions: He intends to love us. He intends to protect us. He intends to bless us and grace us with His presence. He intends to discipline us and correct us. He does not intend to return us to ourselves; He intends to keep us. And His intentions are for us to be in better condition than we were when He got us. All of this God says to us, gently and tenderly, in His Word.

It's difficult to attach much versatility to the mouth of God. It simply speaks. Our mouths smile, but God's mouth doesn't smile in the sense that ours does. His "smile" is a *shining* of His face. Because God is the Source of all joy, He doesn't need to smile; in effect, He *is* a smile. Our mouths eat and chew. His doesn't. He is self-existent and doesn't take anything in, for everything is already in Him. Our mouths kiss and express and emphasize our emotions. God speaks with His.

> WHEN THE MOUTH OF GOD SPEAKS, GOD IS WHAT COMES OUT.

We could be tempted to think that God's mouth is more limited in its operation than ours. But when we consider His words, countless facets unfold before us. Our mouths speak words. God's mouth speaks *His* Word—and He is His Word. Therefore, when the mouth of God speaks, God is what comes out. His words are as creative as He is, as powerful as He is, as life-giving as He is, and as life-changing as He is.

His emotions are wrapped up in His words. Because He is love, the words that He speaks are love. They may not always sound that way to us, but remember, the mouth of God is the revelation of the intentions and priorities of God.

"The mouth of God" is a term that has been used in myriad idioms and metaphors that refer to some dynamic of reaction by God. The phrase "to inquire at the mouth of God" can be found often in Scripture. *To inquire at the mouth of God* is to consult God for His will, His direction, or His guidance. It means *to seek counsel from God.*

The "rod" of the mouth of God speaks of God's divine rebuke.

The "judgment" of God is a manifestation of the wrath of God, most often upon His enemies. "Judgment of God" is a synonym for the law and the word and the will of God.

Several times in Scripture we find the phrase "fire out of the mouth of God," which is representative of the heated anger of God.

There twenty-four instances in the Old Testament where "according to the mouth of God" occurs. Eighteen of those are in the book of Numbers, indicating a heavy concentration of the phrase in the Pentateuch, which is the Torah—the law of God. Those first five books of the Bible contain the most occurrences of "according to the mouth of God." The law was a revelation of God's will and commands, given from His mouth.

There are two broad categories in consideration of the mouth of God: the *speaking* of God's mouth and the *words* of God's mouth. How and why God speaks is indivisible from His words, and His words carry with them the unmistakable stamp of His purpose for speaking.

LET THERE BE!

God is not a silent God. He speaks, and He is speaking. God is "I AM"—continually in the present, the *now*. He speaks actively, continuously, and always with a reason. His mouth is never idle, nor does He engage in useless conversation or insincere sentiment. His reasons for saying what He says are varied, but they all have a common underpinning: to exhibit and express His relationship with His creation.

Genesis 1:1 says, *"In the beginning God.."* The Bible never argues or debates the existence of God. With its very first words, *"In the beginning God,"* the Bible assumes the eternal presence of God. The beginning is the start of something, but in order for anyone to have been there in the beginning, he would have had to be there before the beginning. God never "began"; He always has been. But at a certain point in His eternal existence (and possibly in only a specific dimension), He started a clock called *time*, and set it to ticking.

God's relationship with His creation commenced when He opened His mouth and spoke it into existence. Genesis 1:3 says, *"And God said, Let there be light,"* and light *was*. No debate, no argument. POOF!—light. Whenever God spoke, *"Let there be,"* there *was*.

"Let there be" is such an unimaginable concept that we struggle with it. We strain to embrace the truth that something came out of nothing, simply because the mouth of God spoke it into being. There was nothing—no color, no time, no long or short, straight or curve, measure, depth, direction, even *time or space!* How did He know what to make? How did He know how to make it? There was no language. How did He know what to say when He spoke? There was no expression, only

existence. How did He even know *to* say anything? Why did He not just *do*? Such introspection is overwhelming for our finite little minds. Dwelling on such profundities really strips our gears.

GOD SPEAKS

God created *all* things by His mouth. What is created is always defined by, limited by, and subject to the releases and restrictions placed on it by its creator. God created all things, and He decided what all things were, how they would live, and how long they would live. He created their relationships with each other as well as the boundaries within those relationships. Lions and elephants can live in the same place, but they can't have babies together. Fish can live in water but not for very long on dry land. Some animals can swim, but they can't live underwater. By the word of God's mouth, we cannot converse with a giraffe, but we can speak to each other. God said we would multiply, and we do. All things do what they do because God spoke it thus.

> GOD'S SAYS WHAT HE SAYS TO EXHIBIT AND EXPRESS HIS RELATIONSHIP WITH HIS CREATION.

It is interesting, then, that so much of what He says to us is questioned by us. If God spoke you into existence, does He not know what you can and cannot do? Do you think a cheetah who sees a gazelle ever says, "Nah...forget it. I can't catch 'im. And even if I did, would he let me eat 'im? I think not. I'll dig up some rutabagas instead." Do trees ever worry that they won't bear fruit or that they'll have enough leaves to cover themselves? Doubtful. Yet, I'll bet you probably occasionally question your ability to do what God has already said you can do! Not even considering your ministry, your relationships, or anything else that specific to your life, what about holiness, obedience, or faith? Aren't those spoken from the mouth of God as disciplines we are to pursue? How many times does God have to tell us what He wants us to do before we believe Him—much less simply *do* as He says?

Not only were we brought into being by God speaking His Word, but we also grow in relationship with Him through His Word. His Word enhances our relationship with Him.

> *He that hath my commandments, and keepeth them, he it is that loveth me: and he that loveth me shall be loved of my Father, and I will love him, and will manifest myself to him.* (John 14:21)

The person who has the Word of God and is not only a hearer but a *doer* of it is a person whom Jesus and the Father love. It is this person to whom Jesus promised to manifest Himself. Note the sequence and the progression of the Scripture above:

Know what God said.

Do it.

Jesus then manifests Himself.

The word *manifest* is very important. It means "to shine forth," "to reveal," or "to make visible." It means "to present oneself in the sight of another." It means "to be conspicuous." Jesus said that if we know the Word and obey it, He will become conspicuous in our life. His presence in your life will be obvious when you simply *do* what He says!

To *manifest* also means "to declare," "to speak to," "to make known," and "to make known by speaking." The Bible says that the person who has the Word and *does* the Word will also be rewarded with the blessing of a further word from God.

Some people wait for God to speak about what He has *not* done in their life. But God is waiting for us to do what He has spoken—He says He'll reveal Himself to those who are already walking in obedience to His already-spoken Word.

God never expects us to obey what we don't know to obey. But as we walk in the truth that we have, and as we are obedient to what we already know, then God reveals to us what we don't know, so that we can start doing that as well. He gives us just enough light to take us a little distance at a time. Like a flashlight beam that illuminates only a certain distance into the darkness ahead: You go only as far as the light; and as you move forward, the light moves ahead of you, revealing and lighting your path.

> GOD NEVER EXPECTS US TO OBEY WHAT WE DON'T KNOW TO OBEY.

People who try to take a giant step are going to stumble, because what God wants to show us is in the little steps. Want a wife? Then stop speaking to that woman who's somebody else's wife. Only then can God set you up to receive the revelation of the one who's for you. Want a better job? Then turn off the TV and open the schoolbook after work. When we obey Him, God speaks. When we perform, He promotes us. There is no "automatic pass" in God's educational system. Until we learn the present lesson, we'll keep taking the test over. When we pass fifth grade, He'll move us on up to sixth. But don't ask

God to anoint you for algebra when you won't even do your multiplication tables.

God speaks more as we respond to what He has already said. His speaking is not only to enhance and express relationship; it is also to *involve* us in *relationship with Him*. It is never an accident when God's words reach us—we don't just "happen" to hear the Word of God. It is God's *plan* to engage you with Him. When He speaks, we are expected to listen—*actively*. God considers our hearing complete when we respond properly to what He has said.

On fifteen separate occasions in the New Testament, Jesus said the words, *"He who has ears to hear, let him hear."* Seven of those times occur in the book of Revelation, where He added, *"He who has an ear, let him hear what the Spirit says to the churches."* When His Spirit speaks, He wants us to listen!

Exodus 20 is a great illustration of how most of us think. God had spoken to Moses on Mount Sinai. He had given him the Ten Commandments. These weren't *The Ten Suggestions* or *The Ten Talking Points*. He didn't put a question mark on the end of any of them. When God spoke His law, it was a revelation of His intentions for the people and His instructions to the people.

In Exodus 20, Moses had just come down off the mountain. The people had been looking up at the mountain. They witnessed the lightning flashes, the sound of the trumpet, and the smoke and thunder, and when they saw it, they trembled and shrank back. By the time Moses got to them, they were convinced that God was *serious*.

> *And they said unto Moses, Speak thou with us, and we will hear: but let not God speak with us, lest we die.*
>
> (Exodus 20:19)

These were the chosen people of God, and they didn't want to talk to Him! They wanted the man of God to do it and then relay the messages to them. *Moses, go on up the mountain. Let us know what God said, and we'll do it.* The truth is, they had no plans whatsoever to obey Moses, because every time he had told them what God said to do, they argued with him and murmured against him! But you do have to give them credit: Arguing with Moses was easier than arguing with God, because Moses couldn't zap them into dust!

Some people in the pews make themselves comfortable with some preacher being their Moses. Once every seven days they go find out from someone else what God has to say to them. They don't open their shiny, unsoiled Bibles.

> WHEN GOD SPEAKS, WE ARE EXPECTED TO LISTEN— ACTIVELY.

Some folks have made themselves complacent concerning their relationship with God because they figure that as long as they show up and sit in the seats, the man or woman of God will come down like clockwork from the mountain with a word from God. Part of the reason is that too many churches don't teach people the importance of having a personal, one-on-one relationship with God. Some people don't know that they can go to the throne without permission from their pastor and that God is anxiously awaiting their arrival. And some...they just don't care what God has to say.

Still others are like Israel: They don't want to talk to God because they know that when they do allow Him to speak with them—and them alone—something they're involved with will have to die. You can argue with a pastor. You can debate with a preacher. You can disagree and go on about your business. But once you have a personal, intimate encounter with God, there are some things in your life that He is simply going to kill off. He is not going to allow you into His presence with your sin. And as soon as He tells you that some things in your life will have to die, you can just forget about the next level with Him until you obey.

When there are bad habits, wrong relationships, and sinful behaviors in our lives that we don't want to get rid of, we tend to shy away from closeness with the Word of God. We don't want to get in His presence and have Him come down on us. But there are only two options: You can let the truth of the Word of God begin to kill off those things that hinder your relationship with Him and keep you from being holy, or you can watch the blessings of relationship with Him begin to smother.

Let Him kill your deceitful tongue, or watch your anointing die.

Let Him kill that unsanctified affair, or watch your peace die.

Let Him kill that drug habit, or watch your joy die.

Let Him kill your pride, or watch your vision die.

He's trying to speak life abundant into you. Why trade that for death?

GOD'S WORDS SPEAK LIFE

Go to the mountain yourself and let die what needs to die, and you'll will find God waiting there to show you what He can do in your life. He's not only a God whose word can make life from nothing, He is also the God whose word can make life out of something dead. He's not only the God of creation; He's also the God of resurrection. He is anxious to step into our loneliness and create a love that is anointed by the very word of His mouth. God says that if we let some things die, if we will turn away from them and put our hand in His, He'll lead us to a blessing that He has *already* spoken into being and is there waiting for us!

One of the most amazing things to me about the mouth of God is that it is all-sufficient. Because He is life, His words are life. When He speaks and tells us that He wants some things to die in us and in our life, we don't have to worry that His word won't be enforced: His word will do what needs to be done.

> So shall My word be that goeth forth out of My mouth: it shall not return unto Me void, but it shall accomplish that which I please, and it shall prosper in the thing whereto I sent it.　　　　　　　　　　　　　　　　　(Isaiah 55:11)

Think about the verse above for a moment. God didn't say that Brenda or Jamal or Alfie will do what He says. God's *word* will do what He says! The very ability to do all that God commands is in the command itself; because when God creates, He decides what something or someone is capable of. When He gives a command, the power to complete it is implied.

We are saved and sanctified by the very word of God, who created us through His word. John 1:1 says, "*In the beginning was the Word, and the Word was with God, and the Word was God.*" In Jesus Christ is the *entire* Word of God! He represents God's love for us. If you want to know God as more than a dark, thundering cloud on a mountaintop, then look at the words of His mouth through Jesus. There is no word more romantic than the Word that came forth through, in, and by Jesus. God spoke countless volumes to you personally when Jesus died for you.

God is a God who speaks, presently and continuously. He is never at a loss for words with us. First Peter 1:23 says we have been born again by the incorruptible seed of the Word of God, which lives and abides forever. That means the Word is continually alive in us and dwells in us throughout eternity. The Word is also a *seed*: It needs to be planted, watered, and nurtured in order to grow. Matthew 13 tells us that the seed was sown *in* you, which means the Word is in you. Therefore, the question is *not, Is there a word from the Lord? The question is, Will you hear and obey the Word of the Lord?*

"Do you want to hear God's Word?" is a question of the heart. Jesus said that the condition of our heart is what determines our readiness and ability to hear what has come forth from the mouth of God.

HIS SPOKEN INTENTION

The mouth of God speaks to challenge us, encourage us, transform us, inform us, and comfort us. It speaks to every problem you will ever encounter and every longing you could ever feel. The mouth of God speaks His declaration of intention toward you, His beloved creation.

Awhile ago, my daughter brought a young man home to meet me. She told me he was a preacher like me. He loved the Word like me. When I met him, I did what I always do when I meet the men my daughters bring home: I let him prove his intentions. This is a new millennium; we don't take a young man into the study for cigars to discuss "matters of the heart" anymore. But I wanted to know what this man's intention was with my little girl. So I waited and allowed his actions to speak to me.

One of the proudest moments of my life was having the privilege of performing their wedding ceremony. He had proven that his intentions toward my daughter were good, and I released her with joy.

I did not write this book to entertain you. I don't want to impress you or put on a show for you. I come as a sower who has been blessed with the privilege of sowing the Word of God. It was not by accident that you picked up this book and have read this far. God was not aiming at someone else and accidentally hit you.

I don't believe you're interested in whether or not there is a word from the mouth of Kenneth Ulmer. If you are, then you need to know that my mouth cannot create. My mouth cannot save. My mouth does not sanctify or resurrect from the dead. But my mouth can direct you to God's Word. And He sent me to tell you that His Word, from Genesis to Revelation, is a love letter that outlines His intentions toward you. In prayer and worship, God will emphasize and expound on certain portions and give you a chance to respond as a lover responds to the sweet things that are whispered in the ear. Oh yes, God will whisper to you. In fact, He's waiting for you to ask Him to leave that mountain and come speak to you.

Do you want to hear what God has to say to you personally? If you will ask Him, He will speak!

SEVEN

POWER AND PURPOSE: THE HAND OF GOD

Lord, I am willing
To receive what You give
To lack what You withhold
To relinquish what You take
To suffer what You inflict
To be what You require.
And, Lord, if others are to be
Your messengers to me,
I am willing to hear and heed
What they have to say. Amen.
—Nelson Mink, *Pocket Pearls*

There is probably no metaphor as multidimensional as the workings of the arm, hand, and fingers of God. No other part of the Almighty's anatomy contains as many nuances and facets, and gives as many complex glimpses into His nature, character, and motivations.

That's not surprising when you take a look at human anatomy: The very structure of the arm is comprised of three large bones (the humerus, the ulna, and the radius) that work together to push, pull, pound, and perform, much as the Father, Son, and Holy Spirit work together to achieve Their purposes. The hand at the end of the human arm gropes, grasps, gives, and gathers; while the fingers fulfill the requirements of intricate toil, infinite operation, and intimate expression. Moving further down the arm, activity becomes more specific. Likewise, moving down "the arm of God" to His "hands and fingers," those functions also become more precise and the objects more specific.

And always, the arm, hand, and fingers operate as a unit.

> WHEN WE REFUSE TO CONFESS OUR SINS, GOD WILL ALLOW OUR SITUATION TO HEM US IN UNTIL WE'VE HAD ENOUGH.

In Scripture, the arm, hand, and fingers are sometimes mentioned together, and often the concepts expressed by them are interchangeable. Regarding creation, for example, the prophet Jeremiah said, *"Ah Lord GOD! behold, thou hast made the heaven and the earth by thy great power and stretched out arm"* (Jeremiah 32:17). Jeremiah ascribed God's workings of His miraculous power to His arm.

In Psalm 8:3, King David looked at the same act of God as the work of God's fingers.

When God sent a plague of lice upon Egypt, Pharaoh's magicians called it an act perpetrated by *"the finger of God,"* while God declared that *"the hand of the Lord"* was at work in His plague upon the animals (Exodus 8–9.)

There are aspects of God's behavior that are specific to particular anatomical parts. Although the "arm," "hand," and "finger" are all common biblical images of power, the finger (due to its relative size) carries with it the added connotation of *authority*: It was the finger of God that inscribed the Ten Commandments on tablets of stone (Exodus 31:18). And *"with the finger of God,"* Jesus cast out demons while proclaiming, *"No doubt the kingdom of God is come upon you"* (Luke 11:20).

A person in authority just has to crook a finger at somebody, and they will come. A parent can point and indicate at something, and a child will understand that it means *pick that thing up and bring it here.* My mother could point at me if I was misbehaving in church. Nobody saw that finger but me, but I knew it meant either straighten up or I would get it when I got home—or both! I wonder sometimes why my parents didn't point at me before I started acting up just to let me know they were watching.

The hand of God is unique in its depiction of God's possession and control of something. God's authority is also implied in that image, but the central idea expressed is *possession.* For example, when Jesus declared in John 10:29, *"My Father...is greater than all; and no man is able to pluck* [My sheep] *out of My Father's hand,"* God's authority is stated and assumed, but it is His possession that is being expressed.

It is the consequences of sin that force us under the controlling hand of God. Psalm 32 finds David talking about what some theologians believe was his sin with Bathsheba. He said that when he kept silent about it, he suffered, because (among other things) God's hand was heavy upon him. It is the image of someone trapping us to keep us from moving, and then pressing on us until we cry, "Uncle!"—although in David's case, "Father!" would have been more appropriate.

When we refuse to confess our sins before God, He will allow our sinful situation to hem us in and squeeze on us until we've had enough. Enough pain, enough heartache, enough loneliness, enough shallow living, enough joylessness, enough dry, parched wilderness.

In Psalm 32:4, David said his "moisture" turned to "drought." When we wander or walk away from the living water of God, He will let us get far enough out there, and then He will put His hand on us and *press*. Press long and hard enough on something that is dry, and it will eventually crumble under the pressure. That's why, in his confession and repentance of his sin with Bathsheba in Psalm 51:8, David said, *"Make me to hear joy and gladness; that the bones which Thou hast broken may rejoice."* Talk about pressure—God broke David's bones!

The hand of God is a hand of giving and provision and kindness. But it is also the hand of control: His hand can keep us from continuing in any direction that might destroy us.

The arm of God represents the idea of protection and comfort. This phrase occurs whenever the arm of God is mentioned in the plural. In Isaiah 51:5, the arms of God bring justice to His people. In Deuteronomy 33:27, *"The eternal God is thy refuge, and underneath are the everlasting arms."*

There's an old gospel chorus that declares,

> Leaning, leaning
> Safe and secure from all alarms;
> Leaning, leaning,
> Leaning on the everlasting arms.*

---

* "Leaning on the Everlasting Arms." Words by Elisha A. Hoffman, 1887.

POWER AND PURPOSE: THE HAND OF GOD

The image presented here is that when the arms of God have gathered you up and held you close to the bosom of the Father, there is nothing that can even come close to harming you. You can thumb your nose at the devil from the arms of your heavenly Father and say, "Na na-na-na na! You can't get me!"

The hand of God is rich with revelation about the character of God. His hand represents His power and authority.

Although His arm, hand, and fingers illustrate individual aspects of God's nature, they are usually interconnected in form and function throughout Scripture, so let's examine them as a totality. In the three chapters devoted to this study, "the hand of God" will refer to the arm, hand, and fingers of God. Together, the three emphasize a variety of activities and attitudes concerning God. His is a hand of direction and discipline, provision and protection, giving and guiding.

THE HAND THAT DELIVERS

And the LORD brought us forth out of Egypt with a mighty hand, and with an outstretched arm, and with great terribleness, and with signs, and with wonders.
(Deuteronomy 26:8)

An examination of the story of Israel's deliverance from Egypt reveals a pattern of salvation that is synonymous with our deliverance through salvation in Jesus Christ. There are many references to Moses or Egypt when the New Testament talks about salvation. Back then, as now, the word deliverance conjures in the Jewish mind that specific chapter in Jewish history. When the apostles preached to Jews, the parallel was very useful in bringing them to salvation.

IN *His* IMAGE

The New Testament teaches eternal truths outlined in the Old Testament. When we look at the hand of God and how it functioned for Israel in Egypt, we get a clear understanding of how His hand delivers us today.

> *He hath brought us into this place, and hath given us this land, even a land that floweth with milk and honey.*
>
> (Deuteronomy 26:9)

In the Scripture above, the hand of God brought the Jewish nation out of captivity and into a land flowing with milk and honey. The Bible does not say that He *sent* them out or that He *led* them out, because that terminology would depict a distant God:

AT THE VERY LEAST THE ENEMY HOPES YOU'LL GET BLESSED AND NOT SAY ANYTHING.

If God sends us out, it is like saying that He stays and we go; if He leads us out, then He goes and we follow, as if He's up ahead and we're trotting along behind. While there are significant occurrences of that image in Scripture, in this context God specifically states that He *brought them out by His hand.* And the same hand that brought them out also brought them into the very land that He had promised to give to them as a blessing.

Colossians 1:13 says that God *"hath delivered us from the power of darkness, and hath translated us into the kingdom of His dear Son."* That refers to salvation. It means that when you were saved (when God "delivered" you), He reached for you, picked you up out of your "life before God," and transplanted you into "life with God," all through His Son.

Whenever God takes us out of something, He only does it in order to put us into something better. He never delivers us just to dump us someplace worse to fend for ourselves. It is not God who takes us from better to worse—we do that to ourselves. If *God* has picked you up out of something and it now seems worse to you, then it's only because He hasn't set you down yet; He's just dusting you off. You didn't see all that mess in your life before, because you were in darkness. Once you're in His light, you start to see all that He has delivered you from. When He's done scrubbing and cleaning you off, He'll set you down in something better than He took you out of.

The problem many people have is that they get so caught up in what He's trying to take them out of, that as soon as His hand gets hold of them, they slap it away or try to reach back for what He wants to remove them from. They don't realize that every time they reach back, they miss what He's got for them on the other side. They're settling for *something*, instead of something *better*.

HUSH MONEY

Then there are folks who try to get blessed in the new kingdom while living by the rules of the old. They forget that when God's hand deposited them into His kingdom, they were placed under a new authority. It's like changing jobs: If you were working for Xerox, then got a job working for IBM, you won't get very far working for IBM if your allegiance is still to Xerox! You won't last long if you're still trying to operate according to the rules and procedures of the other company.

Coming to church on Sunday—new kingdom. Meeting that married man for lunch on Monday—old kingdom. Praising God for the blessing of that new house—new kingdom. Cheating on your income taxes—old kingdom.

Too often people don't realize that whenever they are under the authority of the kingdom of darkness, any blessings they receive is the devil's hush money. He tries to pay us off so he can keep us quiet about what's going on in the kingdom of the Son of God. The devil will give us just enough to keep us satisfied and silent. He'll give us a little of this and a little of that, so we won't focus our attention on what's happening over in Jesus' neighborhood. He knows that if we ever find out what God has to offer us in exchange for our faith, we'll stop dancing with the devil in a heartbeat.

The very least the enemy shoots for is that you'll get blessed and you won't say anything about it. Folks living in the kingdom of darkness can't always *see* your blessings from their dark place, but if you proclaim it openly, they will hear you. That's why we can't keep our praise to ourselves when God delivers us. That's also why God wants us to be so blessed with Him that we will *want* to shout, "Hallelujah!"

THE HAND UPRAISED

Look down from thy holy habitation, from heaven, and bless thy people Israel, and the land which thou hast given us, as thou swarest unto our fathers, a land that floweth with milk and honey. (Deuteronomy 26:15)

It was God's hand that brought the children of Israel out, that brought them into their promised land, and that gave them that land—land He had previously sworn to give to them.

God's promising He was going to give the land to the Israelites wasn't some casual remark. It was done "with uplifted hand":

Power and Purpose: The Hand of God

Not one of you will enter the land I swore with uplifted hand to make your home, except Caleb son of Jephunneh and Joshua son of Nun. (Numbers 14:30 NIV)

In the above Scripture, the phrase *"swore with uplifted hand"* is a translation of two Hebrew words: *nasa* ("to be lifted up or raised up") and *yad* ("hand").

God's hand represents His power. His *upraised* hand represents His personal *guarantee* that He will use that power to get done what He's about to promise. And His word is His communication of that pending action.

Before a person testifies in a court of law, they are sworn in. They're asked to raise their hand and solemnly swear to tell the whole truth and nothing but the truth. The raising of the hand is a tradition out of Jewish culture. It is a symbolic gesture that validates the oath or promise being made—it *backs up* the word.

The same hand that pulled Israel out of Egypt and put them in the land and presented that land to them, was the same hand lifted in pledge to their fathers. God had made a promise to their fathers, the patriarchs Abraham, Isaac, and Jacob. Thus, when God is said to have sworn with His uplifted hand, it's not difficult to picture Him standing there with one hand on the Bible (His own Word) and the other hand raised, as if He's about to make a solemn oath before a court. What a powerful image! God Almighty Himself, Creator of the universe and everything in it, giving a solemn pledge before all that He is going to cause something mighty and wonderful to take place on behalf of His children.

Now the LORD had said unto Abram, Get thee out of thy country, and from thy kindred, and from thy father's house,

129

unto a land that I will show thee: and I will make of thee a
great nation, and I will bless thee, and make thy name great;
and thou shalt be a blessing: and I will bless them that bless
thee, and curse him that curseth thee: and in thee shall all
families of the earth be blessed.   (Genesis 12:1–3)

God made a promise to Abraham (who was called Abram at the time) with His upraised hand, to bind the oath. God told him He would bless him and bless others through him. He promised to lead him to a land, give it to him, and make him a great nation, which meant that Abraham's seed would become part of the promise. Abraham—though long dead—would receive the fulfillment of God's promise through his descendants.

He therefore that ministereth to you the Spirit, and worketh
miracles among you, doeth he it by the works of the law, or
by the hearing of faith? Even as Abraham believed God, and
it was accounted to him for righteousness. Know ye there-
fore that they which are of faith, the same are the children
of Abraham. And the scripture, foreseeing that God would
justify the heathen through faith, preached before the gospel
unto Abraham, saying, In thee shall all nations be blessed.
So then they which be of faith are blessed with faithful Abra-
ham.   (Galatians 3:5–9)

When God put us in the new kingdom, we were placed under a different authority, and therefore a different set of rules. In the new kingdom everything operates differently; there's a whole new system of currency. Here, God spells out the rules. The things we used to negotiate and conduct business with in the old kingdom don't work in the new. It's not about our possessions. It's not about our works. The new currency of this new kingdom is *faith*: the thing that now moves things around, gets things done, and causes things to happen. God doesn't move the universe on your behalf because you're so pious or because you follow certain rituals so perfectly. He doesn't help, comfort, guide, and provide for you because of who your mother and father are. He does it solely because of your faith.

God had Abraham's blessing all ready for him; and because Abraham believed that (which is to say that he had faith in God's Word), it activated the promise for him and for his seed, causing the blessing and promise of God to be passed down from one generation to the other. But the passage in Galatians 3 says, *"They which be of faith are blessed with...Abraham."* In other words, the promise that was made to Abraham's seed will go *only* to those who have faith like Abraham!

You might be wondering if that covers you, since you might not be able to trace your family tree all the way back to Abraham. How does a vow made to Abraham's seed affect you? Read a little further through the passage in Galatians, and you'll find out that your family tree has deeper roots than you think:

> Brethren, I speak after the manner of men; though it be but a
> man's covenant, yet if it be confirmed, no man disannulleth,
> or addeth thereto. Now to Abraham and his seed were the
> promises made. He saith not, And to the seeds, as of many;
> but as of one, and to thy seed, which is Christ.
>
> (Galatians 3:15–16)

God made the promise to *"Abraham and his seed."* He didn't say *seeds* plural, but *seed* singular, and that seed is Jesus the Christ. It is Jesus who is the fulfillment of the promise to Abraham's seed.

It is because of God's promise to Abraham, fulfilled in Jesus Christ, that we are now in a position to receive the promise. Galatians 3:27 says that we are sons of God through Christ, because *"as many of you as have been baptized into Christ have put on Christ."* The word *baptize* means "to place, deposit, or immerse into." Salvation took us from one place (darkness) and placed us into Christ. All by the hand of God. Having fulfilled His promise to Abraham through Christ, He now makes us part of that promise by bringing us out of our sin, bringing us to Christ, giving us our land (eternal life), and keeping a promise He made to Abraham long ago.

Galatians 3:8 says God told Abraham that in him *"all nations"* would be blessed. That means it does not matter what the color of your skin is, because God is bigger than your skin. It doesn't matter who your family is, because God is greater than your lineage or your genealogy. He's bigger than your gender, your denomination, your economic circumstances, and your cultural heritage. God keeps every covenant He makes; and He vows that if you belong to Christ, then you're Abraham's seed and *"heirs according to the promise"*!

If I am in Christ, then I am Abraham's seed. And if I am Abraham's seed, then that means when God raised His hand and swore to Abraham, He was swearing to *me*, too. Hallelujah! I now have the right and the divine authority to say, "Lord, whatever You said to Abraham, me too!"

God told Abraham it was time to move from today into destiny. Me too!

He said, "I will make you a great nation." Me too!

"I will bless you." Me too!

"You shall be a blessing." Me too!

POWER AND PURPOSE: THE HAND OF GOD

"I will curse those who curse you." Me too!

The first generation of the children of Israel were not able to go into the Promised Land because they didn't know the delivering, providing, guiding, and giving hand of God. It was not because they had not known the hand of His protection, His power, and His presence. It was because they didn't believe the hand that was raised in promise to Abraham. The people never had a problem believing that God could do anything except keep His word to deliver them into their land.

Never base your entire relationship with God on what you have seen Him do in your life or in the lives of others. Never forget that, above all, God is holy, uncompromising, unfailing *truth.* Hebrews 6:13 says that when God made a promise to Abraham, because there was nothing greater, He swore by Himself. In other words, God raised His hand to Himself and swore an oath to Himself. That is one powerful oath. From God, by God, to God! He was the One who vowed, and He would be the One who would enforce the vow.

> HAVE YOU BEEN CONTENT TO ACCEPT EVERYTHING GOD HAS EXCEPT THE PROMISE YOU CAN'T SEE?

That wasn't enough for the children of Israel. Is it enough for you? You are Abraham's seed. Will you stand on that reality before you step into all that God has for you? Will you believe it when you can't see your way? Will you believe it in spite of your current situation? You know God *can* do anything. Israel knew that, too—that wasn't their problem. Their problem was in believing that He *would* do everything He said He would. They questioned His integrity, questioned His honor, questioned His very holiness. They received everything He mercifully gave them from His hand. But the hand that was raised with nothing in it but a promise...that hand they rejected!

Have you ever done that to God? Have you been content to accept everything God has in His hand except the promise you can't see?

We walk by faith and not by sight. Without faith, it is *impossible* to please God. So we walk (we move forward) by pleasing God, and not by what we see. Faith comes by hearing. What has God told you that you won't hear? It's what you won't hear that stops you from moving forward. He made promises to us in His Word. He vowed some vows to us. He raised His hand to us and said we are fearfully and wonderfully made. Do you believe Him? He raised His hand and said He would never leave you or forsake you. Sure, He chastised you; but before that, His upraised hand promised you that you were His and that His chastisement would yield the fruit of righteousness in you. His hands knitted you together in your mother's womb. But He promised before that to conform you to the image of His Son and make you an heir along with Him.

Do you believe Him even as you struggle to look like His Son? Do you trust that the upraised hand of God means He will keep His word to you? Don't answer too quickly. In fact, let God answer it for you. Ask Him to show you what you believe and what you don't believe. What He reveals might surprise you!

SOVEREIGN HAND OF THE KING

The hand of God is confirmation of the will of God. Moreover, it is simultaneously a confirmation of the sovereignty of God. We will never grasp a clear understanding of the nature of God as it operates through His hand if we don't see that it

134

is always a function of His *sovereignty*. His hand, more than any other part of His anatomy, is the most vivid illustration of it. The hand represents the outward appearance of the will. If you want something, I wouldn't know it until you reached for it. Even if you said you wanted it, your movement toward it is what proves your will. When we see the hand of God in action, it is always confirming three things:

What God wants;

His right to have what He wants;

His ability to get what He wants.

That is *sovereignty*.

The will of God is inextricably tied to the sovereignty of God. That means whatever God wants to do, He has the right and authority to do, as well as the ability to do. So there is never any question that God will have *everything* He desires.

Isaiah 55:11 tells us that God's word will not return to Him void, but will always accomplish what He pleases. His word is His will. And God is the only One who carries out His own will. He doesn't live by the rules—He *is* the rule!

If you know what God wants, that means you know what's going to happen—no ifs, ands, or buts. If you know the will of God, you know that at some point in the future His will is going to be done.

> *For thou art an holy people unto the Lord thy God: the Lord thy God hath chosen thee to be a special people unto himself, above all people that are upon the face of the earth. The Lord did not set his love upon you, nor choose you, because ye were more in number than any people; for ye were the fewest of all people: But because the Lord loved you, and*

because he would keep the oath which he had sworn unto your fathers, hath the LORD brought you out with a mighty hand, and redeemed you out of the house of bondmen, from the hand of Pharaoh king of Egypt. (Deuteronomy 7:6–8)

The passage above gives us a clear image of God's hand as it relates to His sovereignty. Usually, whenever God is speaking to Israel, we can assume that the same principles and patterns apply to us. God said He brought you out of your Egypt because He chose you and loves you. In His sovereignty, God chose you to be a people for Himself, a special treasure set aside just for His pleasure. He made a point to say that you were chosen simply because He loves you.

God's hand brought you out because His will desired it. He, and He alone, deserves credit for your deliverance. He didn't do what He did because of anything you did. His choosing to bless you was a sovereign choice *"because he would keep the oath which he had sworn."* So God brought you out because He loved you, chose you, and desired to keep the oath He made to Abraham. Now think: If the hand of God is an indicator of the will of God, and the hand of God was raised in oath to Abraham (and by extension, to you), then that means that God's oath was His own sovereign choice. He *wanted* to make a promise to you. He *wanted* to love you. His hands made you because He *wanted* to have close fellowship with you.

Many of us have a problem with the sovereignty of God because it takes us completely out of the driver's seat. We can't do anything to earn God's love. We can't make Him love us more or harder or cuddlier. We can't control how His love comes to us. We can't control His choosing. We can't make Him "un-choose" somebody who hurt us. We can't force Him to choose somebody just because we like him or her. It's all up to Him.

"Mighty hand," in Deuteronomy 7:8, refers to the sovereign power that is in God, which in turn speaks to the fact that He decides to bless you. If you want to get technical, God decided to bless you before He even made you.

Revelation 13:8 says that Jesus was the *"Lamb slain from the foundation of the world."* Our sin is no surprise to God. Before we made the choice to sin, He had already decided to bless us with a Savior. He could have tossed you in the trash and made a new you, but He had already made a sovereign choice to make *you* new instead.

Deuteronomy 7:8 says that the Lord redeemed Israel *"from the hand of Pharaoh king of Egypt."* Whenever you see the word *pharaoh* or *Egypt* in Scripture, you can write "the enemy" in your margin. When God sovereignly decided to bless you by bringing you out, He said He had to take you out of the hand of the enemy.

> GOD'S HAND BROUGHT YOU OUT BECAUSE HIS WILL DESIRED IT, AND HE ALONE DESERVES CREDIT.

Remember that old kingdom of darkness from Colossians 1:13? Satan rules that kingdom. When you choose to live there, you live under his rule and authority. But the Bible says God's mighty hand reached into satan's hand and took you out of it. You were in the enemy's hand—you were his possession, under his control. He was doing whatever he wanted to you, with you, and through you. He was trying to block you from receiving the things of God and from living God's will for your life. But God wrapped His mighty hand around your little one, and He snatched you out of the demonic hand that possessed you.

The Word of God says we were taken out of the hand of the enemy. That means three things: First, satan's hand is just a hand, but God's is a *mighty* hand. Whatever satan wants to throw at you, God can block it, or catch it and throw it back harder. When God gets ready to bless you, no other hand is able to stop Him, because His hand is so mighty.

Second, Deuteronomy 7:8 says that God's mighty hand pulled you out of *"the house of bondmen"* (meaning "bondage"). God knew where you were when He decided to bless you. He knew you were bound up and chained to sin. He knew you were in a mess. He didn't wait for you to get out of your mess to bless you—He doesn't bless perfect people; they don't need His blessing. He blesses only those of us who need His blessing. He blessed you by stepping into your bondage, your challenges, your trials and tribulations, taking you by your filthy, scarred, broken hand, and bringing you out.

Third, and most important, if God took you out of satan's hand, the enemy had to know that you were missing! Which means he realized that he had lost you to God. And just in case the devil missed that, David said that God makes every one of His acquisitions very public. David said that when God blesses you, He prepares a table before you and throws a party for you. Now every party begins with a guest list. And this guest list is not complete until He invites all of your enemies so you can sit down right in front of them as God blesses you.

Dear child of God, do not make the mistake of thinking that when you get plucked by the hand of God out of the hand of the enemy that the fight is over for the devil. He still has a few tricks up his sleeve. But they're the same old tricks he's been using since Adam and Eve were trying to find some fig leaves to hide under. His strategy hasn't changed. He talks as much hot air as he can, while he tries to shut you up.

When you're living in sin, the devil is as quiet as a rat. He wants you to make yourself comfortable with him, so he pretty much leaves you alone—unless you get out of hand and start behaving properly. It's not until he finds out that you've left him that he starts shooting off his mouth. He'll tell you you're not really saved. He'll try to convince you that any mistake you make will cause God to revoke His promises to you. He'll tell you to compromise, that God doesn't expect you to be fully holy—after all, that's not realistic these days.

> WHEN GOD PLUCKS YOU OUT OF THE HAND OF THE ENEMY, THE DEVIL'S FIGHT IS NOT OVER.

He just wants you to go to church on Sunday and be a nice person. If you're going to be married one day, it's okay to live together—everybody does that. If you tell people the truth about sin, satan will use the mouths of the people closest to you to tell you that you've changed or you're too judgmental or you're too closed-minded. Or he'll tell you that you are wonderful and holy and anointed and the world loves you! If he can get you puffed up in pride, he won't have to turn you against God; pride will turn God against you.

The best way to deal with the mouth of the enemy is to be ready with God's own words—rooted in your heart and ready on your lips. When Jesus was tempted in the wilderness, He used the truth of the Scriptures against satan. Like

Christ, you need to have a ready word in you at all times. There is something written in God's Word to deal with *everything* that could possibly come your way. The Word is your sword and your shield. Ephesians 6:16 says your shield is your faith; but what you have faith in is the truth of God through His Word.

Imagine the upraised hand of God as your shield against every enemy. Every time we open our mouth with the truth of our testimony or the testimony of our faith, we do damage to the kingdom of darkness. Exodus 13:14 tells us to talk about it whenever the hand of God moves on our behalf. We are told that whenever our children come to us and want to know why we're offering our substance and our thanksgiving to God, we need to respond, *"By strength of hand the LORD brought us out from Egypt."* God said that since He brought us out, we ought to have a testimony about His hand, and that testimony should be passed on to our children and their children.

Never take credit for what God's hand has accomplished in your life. The text implies that when your kids get old enough to realize that they are blessed, when they realize that some of their friends don't live with the peace that exists in your home, don't tell them it's because Mommy and Daddy decided to give them a better life. Don't tell them it's because you pray, you tithe, or you *anything!* Tell them that *the hand of God* brought them the life they have. The hand of God bought the Air Jordans and the food in their bellies. The hand of God fixed the roof and paid the gas bill. The hand of God escorted them home from school when the boy down the street didn't make it past that drunk driver who ran a stop sign. *The hand of God!*

Don't ever steal God's glory.

Power and Purpose: The Hand of God

Nobody but God

Everybody should be able to look at your life and point at some spots that are "nobody-but-God spots." I don't care how smart you are, there have been some things you couldn't think your way out of. There are some things right now that you can't calculate your way out of. You may be driving a nice car, but some of you remember your nobody-but-God bus pass. I like a good filet mignon, but I haven't forgotten my nobody-but-God baloney sandwich days. *Nobody-but-God* could have brought you out of that mess you were in. And nobody but God is keeping you out of another mess.

My favorite nobody-but-God spot is the one that I remember in my prayer closet. Nobody but God could love me enough to take off His deity and come into the filth and sin of this world to rescue me. Nobody but God would die for me for no other reason than that He simply wanted to. That's a hard one to wrap my mind around. Whenever you're faced with the sovereign mercy and grace of God's hand, there's only one way to respond: *Accept it* with great praise and humble thanks!

He chose you because He wanted to. *Accept it.*

He loves you because He wants to. *Accept it.*

Accept His provision, His chastisement, His sunshine, His rain.

Accept the desert He leads you through and the oasis He will surely place in it for you.

Have you accepted God's sovereignty over your life? How much of your life have you thanked Him for?

Acceptance is the proper response to the sovereignty of God demonstrated through the hand of God. True acceptance must always come with gratitude. You might be thinking that you can accept a situation and not be grateful for it. That's not acceptance, that's tolerance. The two are very different. Tolerance affirms only God's power in a situation. Acceptance affirms God's entire *Person*. Tolerance says you believe that God has the ability to do what He's doing in your life; but if you're not also grateful, that means you think there's a better way than God's way. Acceptance says you believe that what He's doing in your life is the wisest, kindest, most loving, most perfect thing that could and should be done for you at that moment.

I find it interesting that God tells us to enter His gates *with thanksgiving* (Psalm 100:4). People don't usually say thank you *before* they receive something. So the fact that God *wants* us to come to Him means His hand has already been active in our life...and for that we should be grateful!

EIGHT

THE GIVING HAND OF GOD

"Daniel Webster was asked, 'What is the greatest
thought that can occupy a man's mind?' He said, 'His
accountability to God.'"
—Abel Ahlquist, *Light on the Gospels*

An idea has taken up residence in my mind, occupying space in the gallery of my thoughts like an exquisite painting. While other notions come and go (some welcome, some not), this one has settled modestly within me. It doesn't have to declare itself to me anymore. It is a fact of my consciousness that appears at very specific moments...

When my son tells a joke, the thought rides on my laughter.

When I look at my beautiful wife, the thought pulls the corners of my mouth into a sly, knowing smile.

The privilege of preaching and teaching the Word is punctuated by the thought, along with the majesty of creation, intimate friendships, the church I pastor, and most of all, my salvation.

The notion that so often adorns my thinking is this: *God has given me so much!*

That may seem obvious to some and trivial to others, but God is never more visible or tangible than when He is *giving*. He sees our needs and hears our cries. When the giving hand of God reaches out to offer provision, guidance, and comfort, He is revealing His compassion to us.

At times I struggle with God's giving hand, especially when I consider how much I have occasionally destroyed, squandered, and mishandled what He has given me. So much of what I have came after second, third, and countless chances.

> WE CANNOT DO WHATEVER WE WANT AND EXPECT THAT GOD WON'T MIND.

When I was a kid we used to have this thing called a *do-over*. If you messed up in a game of Rock, Paper, Scissors, for example, you could say, "Do-over!" and you would get another whack at it. The key was that you were allowed only a certain number of do-overs. After that, you had to live with your goof-ups. No more chances. With God, just when I think I've run out of do-overs, He has mercy on me and gives me another chance.

The apostle Peter thought he ran out of chances after he denied Jesus three times. But when Jesus forgave him and said, "Follow Me," that was Peter's do-over.

Saul was killing Christians until Jesus met him on the road to Damascus, changed his name to Paul, and made him an apostle to the Gentiles. *Do-over.*

THE GIVING HAND OF GOD

The woman at the well, Ruth, King David, and many others were all familiar with the do-over concept.

We cannot do whatever we want and expect that God won't mind. Paul said, "God forbid we become presumptuous enough to take Him for granted!" When I was at the University of Illinois, my first roommate was a guy from a little farm town called Century. He was a believer who liked to listen to country and western gospel music—he even got me hooked on the stuff. One of his favorite songs was "May the Good Lord Never Show You the Backside of His Hand." It was a musical reminder that the giving hand of God can also be His chastening hand!

ABOVE AND BEYOND DELIVERANCE

When I look at the places God's hand has brought me out of and brought me through, I think I would've been satisfied with just deliverance. That was gift enough. But the giving hand of God never settles on just what you need. It goes above and beyond that. Remember, God delivered Israel with a mighty hand from the evil hand of Pharaoh. They had been slaves for more than four hundred years. Simple deliverance would have been something to shout about. No chains and no backbreaking labor would have been reason enough to dance. But God's hand did more than simply deliver. He didn't simply move Hebrews from one end of the desert to another.

THE HOLY BOLD

And the children of Israel did according to the word of Moses; and they borrowed of the Egyptians jewels of silver, and jewels of gold, and raiment: and the LORD gave the people favour in the sight of the Egyptians, so that they lent

*unto them such things as they required. And they spoiled
the Egyptians.* (Exodus 12:35–36)

In the Scripture above, the word *"borrowed"* is sometimes
translated as "asked." Another version says "request." But the
most accurate rendering of the word *borrowed* is "to demand"
or "to demand the right to." It is a very strong word, with an
emphasis on boldness. Moses and his crew went to Pharaoh
and *demanded* a blessing. These were Hebrew slaves, not begging, but *ordering* the Egyptians to hand over silver, gold, raiment, fine linen, and clothing!

What made them so bold? They were not being brought
out of Egypt because they were exceptional in any way. They
knew (and God confirmed it later) that they were not chosen because they were special, but because *God's love for them*
made them special. That's the key. They were bold because
of the God who was with them. The passage says God gave
them favor *"in the sight of"* the enemy. The fact that He gave
them favor doesn't just mean that the enemy saw that they
were favored by God. It actually means that in the eyes of the
enemy, the children of Israel *deserved favor from them!* When
the Egyptians looked at these people who were their slaves,
they looked on them with favor. It wasn't because they were so
wonderful to look at. They were looking at the slaves through
favor-colored glasses, so they not only released them, but they
also blessed them as they went, giving them all of the riches of
the Egyptians! Egypt never recovered her vast wealth—to this
day it remains a Third-World country.

In this scenario, the hand of God gives favor to His people
by putting *His* favor toward them *into the minds of their enemy.*
Remember, these were slaves. In the minds of the Egyptians,

such favor wouldn't make sense. God had to put it there. That's why, after the Hebrew nation had gone and the Egyptians had a chance to think it over, they went after their property (which included their slaves), but it was too late.

When God gets ready to bless us, He'll bless us through folks who don't even know why they're blessing us! It won't make sense to them or to you. Some people are working at jobs they weren't qualified to get, much less keep; but the hand of God gave them favor. There were others with more degrees, more experience and more talent than them, but God granted them favor. The other person's résumé was a mile long. Yours had three little lines. But the blood of Jesus stamped your résumé *FAVORED,* and it was moved to the top of the pile. Some people think that what they really need is a new job or a promotion. No. What they need is the favor of God!

If you have favor, you'll get the job. You know you weren't qualified for that loan. That's why you got turned down so many times. But in God's timing and according to His will, you got that loan because of God's favor. If I ever have a choice between the favor of God and a good credit report, I'll take the favor of God anytime.

If you study the passage in Exodus 12, you'll see the hand of God in another context: Pharaoh ruled the Egyptians, which means when the children of Israel demanded to be blessed, they were making that demand to Pharaoh himself. The hardness of that man's heart was ordained and orchestrated by God (Exodus 4:21). But Pharaoh still consented to release the slaves and bless them as they went.

The king's heart is in the hand of the LORD, *as the rivers of water: he turneth it whithersoever he will.* (Proverbs 21:1)

Pharaoh's heart was in the hand of God the way the rivers are. Rivers are different from other bodies of water in that they move from one place to another. They do not form themselves; rather, they are formed when outside forces act on them. Snow melts from a mountaintop, and the water, obeying the laws of gravity, runs down and cuts a river for the water to flow through. Eventually rivers empty into other bodies of water. The point is that the river is not in control of its beginning or its end. It turns and flows according to its origin and destination. Pharaoh's heart was subject to the hand of almighty God, so that when God was ready to grant His people favor, Pharaoh could do nothing but comply.

> GOD WILL OFTEN BLESS US THROUGH FOLKS WHO DON'T EVEN KNOW WHY THEY'RE BLESSING US.

Psalm 105 says God brought them out with silver and gold, and adds in verse 37, *"There was not one feeble person among their tribes."* They were not only delivered, but they also were healed and made whole! They didn't come out of Egypt moaning and broken. They came out strong and able so they could make the journey ahead. God's hand had given them favor, and then riches, and finally health and wholeness.

They had been working so hard in Egypt that the Bible says they cried out, and their cries reached God in heaven. And these people, who had known nothing but backbreaking labor, were miraculously healed of every infirmity and disease. There were no achy joints, cuts, or bruises. The weak were strengthened and the lame walked. God knew the journey they were about to undertake, and He prepared them for it with health, healing, and riches.

But wait...why riches? They were headed for the wilderness. There were no stores in the wilderness; no Wasteland Wal-Mart. They carried fancy clothing, but there were no banquets planned for the wilderness excursion. Even today, there are no malls in that wilderness. Why did they need such wealth? They would be in the wilderness for forty years with no place to spend any of it. They didn't know they would be there for forty years, but God certainly did. The book of Numbers tells us that their clothes didn't wear out in the wilderness, so why did they need to bring all the luxurious linens and fabrics, not to mention the jewels?

God is not wasteful or frivolous. He did not give the children of Israel wealth to have a fashion show in the desert. He gave it for a reason:

> *And the LORD spake unto Moses, saying, Speak unto the children of Israel, that they bring me an offering: of every man that giveth it willingly with his heart ye shall take my offering. And this is the offering which ye shall take of them; gold, and silver, and brass, and blue and purple, and scarlet, and fine linen, and goats' hair, and rams' skins dyed red, and badgers' skins, and shittim wood, oil for the light, spices for anointing oil, and for sweet incense, onyx stones, and stones to be set in the ephod, and in the breastplate. And let them make me a sanctuary; that I may dwell among them.*
>
> (Exodus 25:1–8)

In the wilderness they were preparing to build a tabernacle as a dwelling place for the Lord. God told Moses to take up an offering to build His house. That's the reason the hand of God filled their hands with blessings—so they would give some of it back to Him. Not all of it. Notice He said, "Take up

149

an offering," not "Give Me back all the stuff I gave you." He could have. The book of 1 Chronicles says that all we have to give came from God in the first place.

In the wilderness they were preparing to build a tabernacle as a dwelling place for the Lord. God was calling on the people to give their time, talent, and effort, along with their substance. The riches they took out of Egypt would be used in God's dwelling place, along with the labor of the people to build it. Exodus 35:10 called for the participation of every *"wise hearted"* person. The *New Living Translation* says every *"gifted craftsman"* was called into service.

I love how the verse says *"every"* skilled person among them should come and work. Most churches today are short-handed because too many "skilled craftsmen" are just warming the pews. God called everyone who could work. The Bible says in Exodus 35 that everybody from blacksmiths to seamstresses worked and gave so that the temple of the Lord could be built. And the purpose of building the tabernacle was to house His presence. He wanted to dwell among His people, so He blessed them with the provision to build a place in which He could show up.

God wants to be close to His people. He wants to be seen by His people and with His people, so that ultimately He can dwell *in* His people:

> *Know ye not that ye are the temple of God, and that the*
> *Spirit of God dwelleth in you?* (1 Corinthians 3:16)

The people gave in order to prepare for His presence to dwell in the tabernacle of the desert of their deliverance. If we want God to show up not just in our life but *in us*, then we must understand the importance of giving. This is not a principle about money (though it certainly includes material things); it's about giving. Giving creates an atmosphere of revelation—not the revelation itself, but the atmosphere. The giving does not make God come. You can't purchase the blessings of God. The offering prepares *a place* for God to come. The Bible says that when the tabernacle was finished, a cloud covered the tent and the glory of the Lord filled the tabernacle so that not even Moses could go in:

> *The cloud of the LORD was upon the tabernacle by day, and fire was on it by night, in the sight of all the house of Israel, throughout all their journeys.* (Exodus 40:38)

The giving heart prepares an accommodation for the revelation of the glory of God. That principle plays itself out throughout Scripture. In 1 Kings 17 for example, the widow in Zarephath barely had anything to eat. In fact, she had just enough flour and oil to make what the Word says was to be the last meal for the widow and her son before they died.

The prophet Elijah, however, told her to make a little cake for him first. Now, if I had been that widow, I would have thought, *This mighty prophet has no shame in asking a poor widow to cut her last supper in half so he can eat—and to top it off, he tells me to feed him first!* I would have had a little talk with the great prophet. "Look, 'Lij, I have only enough to feed me and my little boy. Have a heart—there's a famine going on here, brother!"

But the Bible says she made the cake and gave it to the prophet. Period. No argument. No discussion. No moaning or carping. Her giving attitude brought God on the scene...and her flour and oil didn't run out for over a year! Supernaturally, every time she went to pour out some oil, there was more oil.

Supernaturally, every time she went to get a little meal and thought she was at the bottom of the barrel, there was more meal. She gave what God asked for, and God showed up.

Notice I said she gave what God asked for, not what the prophet asked for. The only reason Elijah the prophet showed up in Zarephath was because God told him to go there and there would be a widow, *"whom I have commanded...to sustain thee"* (1 Kings 17:9). The word *"commanded"* doesn't mean that God had already told the woman to take care of the prophet. It is a word that means "appointed" or "ordained." In other words, God had already ordained that the woman would give Elijah what he asked for.

The hand of God has blessed you. And He has earmarked some of what He has blessed you with for you to give back into His hand. He has already decided where it should go and when. He knows what church you go to and who among your friends needs to be blessed specifically by you. He has given you time, talent, and treasure. He has made you ready to give. Your job is to be *willing*. When we give under those conditions, we can count on the blessing of His presence.

> GOD WANTS TO BE SEEN BY HIS PEOPLE AND WITH HIS PEOPLE, SO THAT HE CAN DWELL IN HIS PEOPLE.

All day and every day, the Lord was with Israel. But Israel never understood the principle that God taught them about giving. They constantly turned away from God and gave their offerings to idols, and God withdrew from them. They looked for the hand of God to rescue them, provide for them, and guide them, but they missed what God was trying to teach them through His example of giving. So, He would often allow them to handle things on their own—until that got them into trouble. Then, when they called on Him, confessed their sin, and humbled themselves, He would restore them to right relationship with Him. Yet, they would slip back into their old ways again and again.

It's about Revelation

Behold, I send My messenger, and he will prepare the way before Me. And the Lord, whom you seek, will suddenly come to His temple, even the Messenger of the covenant...."Behold, He is coming," says the LORD of hosts. But who can endure the day of His coming?...For He is like a refiner's fire and like launderer's soap....He will purify the sons of Levi, and purge them as gold and silver, that they may offer to the LORD an offering in righteousness.

(Malachi 3:1–3 NKJV)

Israel had always waited for the coming revelation of the Messiah. Malachi said Messiah is coming. God said He's preparing the way for Him to come. But Malachi said some folks weren't ready for Him. God said that the Messiah's coming would be a problem for some because they could not stand in His coming. When He comes, there would be a purifying going on that would separate the righteous from the unrighteous.

"I do not change; therefore you are not consumed, O sons of Jacob. Yet from the days of your fathers you have gone away from My ordinances and have not kept them. 'Return to Me, and I will return to you,' says the LORD of hosts. But you said, 'In what way shall we return?'" (Malachi 3:6–7 NKJV)

God said that Israel was not ready for His blessing because they had not kept His commandments. The text implies that they had been repeatedly disobedient. This wasn't a one-time offense. Their sin was a lifestyle. It was their pattern. Normally, God would have consumed them, just wiped them out. But He had made a promise to them long ago. He had raised His hand to them and made an oath. He had told them that they were His chosen people, and no matter how far they got from Him, as long as they repented of their sins and returned unto Him, He would not destroy them. He promised to restore their relationship with Him if they would return. So He said, "You're lucky I'm a God who keeps His word and does not change. Otherwise, I'd be pouring out wrath instead of mercy, and you'd be toast."

He told them to return to Him, but the text tells us that Israel didn't know how. They asked, *"In what way shall we return?"* And God answered:

> *Will a man rob God? Yet you have robbed Me!*
> (Malachi 3:8 NKJV)

Huh?? That answer went right over their heads. Here they were talking about being prepared, about receiving the coming Messiah, about getting ready for the revelation of the Lord and how that revelation would usher them into a new dimension in God's will. They were talking about a new unveiling of a part of God's divine purpose for them, so they asked Him how they could be prepared, and His answer is, *"Will a man rob God? Yet you have robbed Me!"* Where'd that come from—did God not understand their question?

God had told them that they had been lax concerning His law. They asked how, and God answered with something they either didn't hear or didn't understand. So Israel responded, "In what way have we robbed You, Lord?!"

The Giving Hand of God

I love God. He's so specific when He talks to us, that there's no confusion. You can take something by accident; but when you rob someone, you do it deliberately. God told them they had robbed Him. He didn't say they accidentally took something from Him, or even that they mistakenly took something that they thought belonged to them. He said, "Israel, you robbed Me!" He didn't bite His tongue. He didn't stutter. He spelled it out. He let them know that they robbed Him in tithes and offerings. Yet, this was *not actually about the tithes and offerings!* Remember, they began this conversation talking about Israel's readiness to see the revelation of God. He told them they were not ready. They asked what they could do to get ready, and in reply He asked a rhetorical question to get them to see how serious this business of giving is.

When God said, *"Will a man rob God?"* that was appalling to them because God was accusing them of something that could get them *killed*! He had just told them that the only reason they weren't consumed was because they were His chosen people. They did not understand that from the time the hand of God brought them out of Egypt, He had put into action a spiritual cycle of *preparation, expectation, and revelation.*

They asked God how to receive His presence. And He told them what was standing in the way of it. He did not mention fornication. He did not say, "Adultery!" He didn't say anything about backbiting or covetousness. He said the thing that made them unprepared was their *lack of giving!* And that therefore they wouldn't be ready to receive the revelation of Jesus Christ, the Anointed One. Stunning! And they really didn't get it.

The text is not so much about rebellion as it is about a lack of understanding. It's not that they didn't understand that they had held back their tithes and offerings; it's that they didn't understand how serious that crime was.

But if it wasn't their money, then why was God's solution for Israel to *give*? Why did He tell the Israelites, in Malachi 3:10, to bring the tithes they had robbed Him of into the storehouse? In order to understand what God was trying to communicate to them (and to us), we have to look at the entire verse:

> *"Bring all the tithes into the storehouse, that there may be food in My house, and try Me now in this," says the* LORD *of hosts, "If I will not open for you the windows of heaven and pour out for you such blessing that there will not be room enough to receive it."* (Malachi 3:10 NKJV)

This is the pattern of preparation, expectation, and revelation. God said to bring all the tithes to the storehouse. The temple was maintained and the priests were fed by the tithes and offerings that were brought into it. If the people were not giving, the work of the ministry suffered. So, giving prepares the house of the Lord.

Then God said, "Give and expect Me to pour out a blessing you won't have room to receive." That is expectation. God tells us to first bring your tithe, and then we can expect Him to do some things. That's important because that expectation is your act of *faith*. *"Faith is the substance of things hoped for, the evidence of things not seen"* (Hebrews 11:1). When we give, God says we ought to expect Him to keep His Word to us about what happens when we give. He said He would pour out a blessing. The phrase *"pour out"* means "to empty out." God plans to keep pouring until the blessing He has for you is completely out of heaven and in your hands. And He said we wouldn't even have room enough to receive it! We can receive material things, so He can't be talking about that. The only thing God could pour out that we don't have room to receive is *Himself*. That's the revelation! The presence of God awaits any man or woman with a heart that is willing to give.

Most of us look at that text and our minds automatically go to the tithe. But the grammatical structure of the sentence suggests that the emphasis is on the *act of giving*. In *"bring all the tithes,"* the word *bring* is actually the emphasis of the sentence. God wants us to bring to Him what belongs to Him; but we're blessed by the *bringing*, not by the tithe. The tithe is for the upkeep of His house, where He dwells with His people. The bringing is what causes the windows of heaven to open. The way we know that is in the question, *"Will a man rob God?"* Remember, the problem is the

> GOD IS SO SPECIFIC WHEN HE TALKS TO US THAT THERE'S NO CONFUSION.

robbery. That word *rob* means, in the original Hebrew, "to cover up something." The picture is of a person who puts his hand over the opening of a chalice or a cup to hide or withhold the contents. The people had robbed God by putting their hands over their tithes and offerings, which belonged to God. That was a serious offense.

Hundreds of years later, the writer of the book of Acts showed us exactly how serious. The New Testament church was being formed. Like the children of Israel, believers in that day were in a season of giving for the purpose of building the ministry. Acts 4:32 says the people were *"of one heart and of one*

soul," and they gave willingly wherever there was a need. But one couple got a little selfish:

> *There was also a man named Ananias who, with his wife, Sapphira, sold some property. He brought part of the money to the apostles, but he claimed it was the full amount. His wife had agreed to this deception. Then Peter said, "Ananias, why has Satan filled your heart? You lied to the Holy Spirit...How could you do a thing like this? You weren't lying to us but to God." As soon as Ananias heard these words, he fell to the floor and died....About three hours later his wife came in, not knowing what had happened. Peter asked her, "Was this the price you and your husband received for your land?" "Yes," she replied, "that was the price." And Peter said, "How could the two of you even think of doing a thing like this—conspiring together to test the Spirit of the Lord? Just outside that door are the young men who buried your husband, and they will carry you out, too." Instantly, she fell to the floor and died...They carried her out and buried her beside her husband.*
>
> (Acts 5:1–5, 7–10 NLT)

You may think you're only affecting the church's account when you don't give, but it's much more serious than that. Peter said you aren't keeping anything from your pastor; you're defrauding *God* Himself! He may not strike you dead, but there's a good chance that some areas of your life that should be flourishing may be dying instead. The violation of Ananias and Sapphira was not in the amount they gave. It was in their holding back something that belonged to God. They hid something that should have been given to God—and then they had the added gall to lie about it!

Obviously, when you put your hand over a cup, it keeps the contents away from others. But it also keeps anything from being poured *into* the cup as well. When you rob God, you keep Him from being able to bless you. He desires to bless you, but He can't because your own hand is in the way. That's why God said the people were cursed in Malachi 3:9. Part of His promise to His people was that He would bless those who blessed them and that He would curse those who cursed them. If you bless the chosen people of God, you get blessed. If you curse them, you get cursed. There's no in-between. This rule applies to the chosen people themselves as well. When God's chosen people prevent God from blessing them, they are forcing God to curse them.

God was not asking Israel for money. What He wanted was a giving heart, an attitude of willingness to give. As we lay the pattern of God's command to give onto our own lives, our focus should not be on the money. God does not ask you to give Him anything that He didn't already give you in the first place. If you have ten dollars, He's not going to ask you for twenty. If you are a gifted singer, He's not going to ask you to devote your time to playing guitar in the church band. If you have no compassion in your heart, He'll do what He has to do in order to give you compassion—and *then* He'll ask you to give compassion.

> GOD'S GOAL IS TO DWELL IN THE TEMPLE OF HIS PEOPLE.

We're so stingy with God. We have no right to treat Him like He's making an imposition on us. We look at Him like we want to say, "Why are You asking me for that? Haven't You seen my bank account?!" Yes, He has seen it. And everything in it, *He* put there. If He asks you to give it, you can say you don't want to, but don't tell Him you don't have it. He can work on our heart only when we're honest with Him. But when we look Him in the eye and lie, we've just cut off the hand of his giving to us. And maybe worse.

God does not need our money. If He needs money, He can make some. God will build what He wants, feed as many as He wants, and reach whomever He wants to, with you or without us. He could build a ten-million-dollar sanctuary with twenty million people giving fifty cents apiece if He had a mind to.

Some people wonder why God talks so much about giving; and why He commands us to give, as opposed to leaving it up to us whether we want to give or not. It is because the purpose of giving is to see the glory of God. When we give, God says we can expect Him to show up. And when He does, we'll see His glory. Where will we see His glory? In His temple: us! According to 1 Corinthians 3:16, *we* are God's temple!

God's goal is to dwell in the temple of His people. If God is dwelling in the temple, then He should be visible. In other words, if He is dwelling *in us*, then we should look like Him. Our eyes should see like His do. Our ears should hear like His do. We should reflect His holiness. Our arms should be willing to reach out to lost souls. Our hearts should be loving like His. And *our hands should be giving, like His hands give*.

Hands that cover up what belongs to God do not glorify God. When God says, "You have robbed Me," He's talking about His *glory*. God is the supreme Giver. His love is expressed in giving. He so loved the world that He *gave* His Son. Then His Son *gave* His life for us. And we are told to give, because God desires to replicate Himself in us. Giving makes

God visible to the world—through us. The reason God loves a cheerful giver is because He's a cheerful Giver. It is His good pleasure to give to His children out of His own hand.

It took me awhile, but I finally got it: God doesn't want His money back; He wants His glory. God is a Giver of the most glorious kind. One of the most magnificent facets of His personality is His generosity. There is no part of Him that doesn't give. He can't help it. In fact, God could not receive anything from us that would increase Him because He can never become more than He already is. That means He doesn't even need the glory that we give Him. If we don't glorify God in our giving, He is no less glorious. If we do, He's no more. Think about that. Even the glory is for *our* benefit. He's not changed by it, we are! He only wants His glory *for what it gives to us.*

There's that thought again, flitting across my mind. *God has given me so much.* All that I have He has given to me. All I give glorifies Him but changes me, so all that I give gives back to me. Oh, that my hands would become the hands of God, anxious to give and not thinking long on what is given back, except on how to transform it into another gift...for *His* glory!

NINE

THE POTTER HAND OF GOD

> "Life is a grindstone. Whether it grinds you down or polishes you up depends upon what you are made of."
> —James S. Hewett, *Illustrations Unlimited*

*W*e have looked at the hand of God that blesses, rescues, gives, guides, protects, and keeps. Those images of God cause us to shout the roof off because they mean we are blessed, saved, receiving, secure, not lost, and not alone. However, there is another, not-so-comfortable aspect of God's hand that is difficult for many of us to deal with...

In Acts 20:27, Paul told the Ephesians, *"I have not failed to declare unto you the whole counsel of God's Word."* Too many preachers today have diluted the Word of God to such a degree that they do little more than tickle the ears of God's people. The contemporary church has moved into such a "bless me" mode that leaders are often fearful and hesitant to declare the whole counsel, in particular that part of God's Word that doesn't "feel good." Paul told the Ephesians that he had not failed to say all there was to be said, not just the nice things that people would be comfortable with.

The hands of God are hands that shape and mold us according to His will. In this context, we appeal to the Creator and Designer in Him. God is the Potter, skillfully working out His will through us, His "lumps of clay."

> *The word which came to Jeremiah from the* Lord, *saying, Arise, and go down to the potter's house, and there I will cause thee to hear my words. Then I went down to the potter's house, and, behold, he wrought a work on the wheels. And the vessel that he made of clay was marred in the hand of the potter: so he made it again another vessel, as seemed good to the potter to make it. Then the word of the* Lord *came to me, saying, O house of Israel, cannot I do with you as this potter? saith the* Lord. *Behold, as the clay is in the potter's hand, so are ye in mine hand, O house of Israel.*
>
> (Jeremiah 18:1–6)

Adelaide A. Pollard picked up the theme of Jeremiah 18 and said, humbly and submissively:

> Have Thine own way, Lord!
> Have Thine own way!
> Thou art the potter, I am the clay.
> Mold me and make me after Thy will,
> While I am waiting, yielded and still.

God as Potter is the picture of deepest intimacy and closest contact with the believer. His are the hands that handle us and therefore know us through the familiarity of touch. That can be a comforting image until we consider that the hands of a potter desire to go beyond tracing the outline of the clay as it is. The constant goal of the potter is to improve the shape of the clay He is working.

THE POTTER HAND OF GOD

The potter hands of God seek to change us into something besides what we were when we came to Him. That is where discomfort begins: with the declaration of God that we are not what He would have us to be. That's not easy for people to hear. It messes with the ego and deflates self-confidence.

When you buy clay from the store, it comes in a block—a nice, neatly packaged, pretty, sensibly shaped block. Some people build nice block lives, all neat and orderly. Then they find themselves in the hands of the Potter, and the first thing He does is to pound the shape away. Nothing is neat anymore. That wonderful, clear, protective plastic has been removed and discarded. The block is now an unattractive lump, and all recognizable things have been bludgeoned away by the fist of the Artist who has something in mind but hasn't bothered to inform us of what it is. Welcome to the hand of God.

> DISCOMFORT BEGINS WITH GOD'S DECLARATION THAT WE ARE NOT WHAT HE WANTS US TO BE.

There are two very important things we need to know as we seek to submit ourselves to the idea of God as the divine Potter. First, every great artist knows what he's making before he starts working. God already knew His plans for you before His hands made contact with you. One of the first things God told Jeremiah was that his life was no accident. Jeremiah's birth was not a fluke generated by haphazard human interactions and passions. It was purposed in the wisdom of the sovereign mind of God. God is not trying to decide what He's going to do with you. He made you only because He knew what you would be. The hand of God is confirmation of the will of God. That means He willed you before He made you.

165

Before I formed thee in the belly I knew thee; and before thou camest forth out of the womb I sanctified thee, and I ordained thee a prophet unto the nations. (Jeremiah 1:5)

Second, you should know that God knows *how* to do everything He wants to do with you. That's just as important as Him knowing what He wants to do with you, but it's not always as obvious.

MARRED VESSELS

The following verse grips me every time I read it, because it says the vessel that the potter was making was *marred in his hand.*

And the vessel that he made of clay was marred in the hand of the potter: so he made it again another vessel, as seemed good to the potter to make it. (Jeremiah 18:4)

Something doesn't sit quite right with me in the notion that the vessel the potter made was marred in his hand. He made it. It's not a vessel he got from someone else's shop; it was one that was made with his hand, and the verse says it was *flawed.* It might have made sense if someone else had made it and put it in his hand already marred, but that's not what the text says. It says the vessel *he made* was marred *in his hand.* And when he recognized that it was damaged, he made it again into another vessel *"as seemed good to the potter to make it."*

The potter is God.

The clay is us believers, God's people.

The Potter's wheel is God's method of expressing His will in our lives. The will, the design, the desire of the Potter is worked out on the Potter's wheel, which is our *destiny.*

The *shape* of the vessel is God's will for our lives.

But here is a piece of pottery that God made with *His* hands...and it's flawed! That is nearly impossible to comprehend. And yet, it is *good* for us, because His mysterious process always leads to perfection.

The word *marred* means "not suitable to be used." It means "messed up," a piece of pottery in the Potter's hand that is not suitable to be used. *Marred* also means "worthless, without value." And that is our hope, because normally if a potter made something that was flawed, he would cast it aside. But we don't have *a* potter working on us, we have *the* Potter working on us! The text doesn't say the vessel is cast aside. It says that the Potter kept it in His hand and made it into something even better.

But the question I wrestle with is, "What happened to the clay in the first place that marred it?" Did something happen in the making process that damaged it? Was the clay damaged before the potter got his hands on it?

When the Potter put the clay on the wheel and started to work, it was with His will in mind. God, the Potter, was making something. He wasn't just playing around with some clay. He was working intentionally and deliberately when He sat down at the wheel. He had an idea of what that clay was to look like when He was finished working, so that His will would be manifested on the wheel and made resident in the clay.

Here is what the Potter was thinking when He got the clay:

> *For I know the thoughts that I think toward you, saith the* LORD, *thoughts of peace, and not of evil, to give you an expected end.* (Jeremiah 29:11)

One version of the passage above says *"to give you a future and a hope."* When the Potter sat down at the wheel, His will was that the pottery He makes might end up in a peaceful place. His thoughts of you, His ideas, His plans for your life are plans of peace and not evil. He does not plan for your end to be evil, but that you would have hope and a future. So what happened in the middle that caused so many problems that we wound up in His hand marred and scarred? Well, perhaps He made it and something happened to it, and when He picked it up again, it was marred.

Let's look at the example of King David. Psalm 31 is a psalm of David, the words of which were also quoted by Jesus. David said, "I put my life in Your hand, Lord. I put my spirit in Your hand," which is a good place to be.

> *Into thine hand I commit my spirit: thou hast redeemed me,*
> *O LORD God of truth.* (Psalm 31:5)

But what condition was David in when he put himself in God's hand? Verse 12 tells us:

> *I am forgotten as a dead man out of mind: I am like a broken*
> *vessel.* (Psalm 31:12)

Another translation says, *"I am like a piece of broken pottery."* And another renders the phrase as, *"a discarded pot."* Clearly, David felt worthless and broken. He put his spirit into God's hand and he felt like broken pottery. He said, "I put myself in Your hand, but I feel like I am nothing."

You will meet people day in and day out with smiles on their faces covering up broken and shattered hearts. Once when I was in South Africa, I heard a report on television that there was a rape in South Africa *every twenty-six seconds!* South Africa was the rape capital of the world. Three out of four women there would be raped before they turned sixteen. South Africa is a country of broken and abused women.

Did something happen in your life that made you feel broken and discarded? What has occurred that made you feel worthless? Did someone or something damage you? What happened that cracked your beauty or marred your self-esteem? David felt like a dead man, like he was going out of his mind. He felt totally forgotten and thrown away like a shattered vase, useless and worthless.

Life can break us, can't it? Sometimes we go to God with our wounds, and in our brokenness, when we place ourselves in His hand, we think we are putting "nothing" in His hand, because we feel like nothing. We look in the mirror and see nothing looking back at us. David felt like a broken pot. But even with his brokenness, David said, "I'm in God's hand."

> OUR RELATIONSHIP WITH GOD IS A TWO-WAY STREET.

I cannot tell you the number of times I have felt worthless. I cannot tell you the number of times I've felt like a failure, or felt useless. My only consolation was found in the knowledge that I was in God's hand.

The Bible says that the Potter held the pot and that the pot was marred. We are never told what specifically marred the pot, but the next verse says that because it was marred, the Potter did something very interesting: He *made it again*. In order to make it again, He had to put it back on the wheel. In fact, He would have had to crush it first. It was already damaged, but in order to make it over again, He would have to reduce it back to the clay it was before it was pottery, and then put it back on the wheel to make it over again.

You think, *Wait a minute. I just went through something, and You're going to put me back up on that wheel? I've been through hell and high water, and in order to bless me, You're going to crush me? I already feel like nothing. I feel worthless; and in order to make me over, You are going to start this process all over again?!* But just remember Jeremiah 29:11: His plans for you are to give you peace and a future and a hope! That means that, as painful as things are, they will eventually lead to that expected end. The hands of God work only according to the will of God.

A BATTLE OF WILLS

The damage done to the pot could have happened without the pot's permission. But there is another implication that gives insight into how the vessel was marred in the Potter's hand. The text suggests to us that the scars and the marring may not be because of what someone did to the pot, for we see that the clay *has a will of its own* and has the ability to resist the will of the Potter.

As you continue to read through Jeremiah 18, you'll discover that the clay (God's people) have rebelled and disobeyed Him. So maybe we don't have to feel so sorry for every piece of marred pottery. If you keep reading, you find that Israel had disobeyed God and that the marring of their vessel was related to their sin. The brokenness and flaws were a product of the choices they made. The Bible says they turned against God, and in so doing they missed out on the blessings He would have had for them.

But He would make the vessel over again, implying that He would have to crush it and break it, an implication that God is acting out of anger. The remaking of the pot is an expression of God's displeasure with it, and because He's not pleased, He'll make it over, instead of letting it remain as it is. If it means a painful pounding down, then He'll do that in order to get it to where He wants it. This is not a tender remaking or rebuilding. It is God's chastisement, which, while it is a function of His mercy and grace, is neither comfortable nor painless. But He will do with us as He wills—even when some people seem to question God's right to make them over.

> *O house of Israel, cannot I do with you as this potter? saith the* LORD. *Behold, as the clay is in the potter's hand, so are ye in mine hand, O house of Israel. At what instant I shall speak concerning a nation, and concerning a kingdom, to pluck up, and to pull down, and to destroy it; if that nation, against whom I have pronounced, turn from their evil, I will repent of the evil that I thought to do unto them. And at what instant I shall speak concerning a nation, and concerning a kingdom, to build and to plant it; if it do evil in my sight, that it obey not my voice, then I will repent of the good, wherewith I said I would benefit them.*
>
> (Jeremiah 18:6–10)

Our relationship with God is a two-way street. He says that if those who've turned against Him will repent, then He'll return to them and bless them the way He promised in the beginning. But if He declares a blessing and they turn away from Him, then they have forfeited all rights to the blessing. In essence, our disobedience tells God that we don't want Him to bless us, so He withholds blessings from us and will chastise us until we learn to desire His blessing. God loves us, but

He will "spank" us if we need it. Modern parents can't seem to relate to that. God is not going to give you a "time out" in the corner. He's not going to wag a finger and talk to you. He's talked through sixty-six books worth of Bible, sermons, friends, circumstances, and even directly to you in prayer. When He's done talking, He's done. And there's no use getting all bent out of shape about it. It's standard in our salvation contract:

> *And ye have forgotten the exhortation which speaketh unto you as unto children, My son, despise not thou the chastening of the Lord, nor faint when thou art rebuked of him.*
> (Hebrews 12:5)

God is not playing around. He is serious as He is making something out of you, laboring and working with His clay. Many people think that God is not really all that serious. They go to church Sunday after Sunday but live any way they want to live Monday through Saturday. That's because they believe God is too loving to be a disciplinarian. Too many people don't live their lives with the constant awareness that they are in the hands of an almighty sovereign God. They go from one healing line to another, from one crusade to another, and between the crusades and the healing they live the way they want to. Some have "repented" of the same thing so many times that they don't even feel bad about it anymore. It's just a routine.

The book of Hebrews says that God will spank His children. And He says, "Don't run away when it's your turn." God tells us not to faint when He rebukes us. That's a strange one.

When I was young and it was time for us to get a spanking, my mother would wait in one spot. We'd run around the house and down the street, and she would just wait because sooner or later we'd have to come home. I remember a time when Mama hadn't even laid a hand on my sister Kathy. She just drew back her hand and Kathy started hollering. Mama said, "I haven't even touched you yet."

God hasn't even spanked some people yet, and they're ready to fall apart. What are they going to do when He actually does make contact? The Scripture tells us not to fall out when God rebukes us, and don't run away when it's our turn to get a spanking.

Discipline in our house was always made worse by the fact that we were forced to participate in our own pain. We had these trees in our yard, and when it came time for punishment, my parents made us go out and get the switch they were going to use on us. We had two trees. One was a willow, and the other one had long, thick, wiggly branches.

> TOO MANY PEOPLE AREN'T AWARE THAT THEY ARE IN THE HANDS OF AN ALMIGHTY GOD.

Mama would say, "You go get a switch." We had to pick your own instrument of destruction! There I was outside, pulling on branches from a tree, testing them for their pain potential. The problem was, you couldn't come in with something that was obviously not going to hurt you. I got more "double whippings" for bringing in little skinny wisps of willow than I'd like to remember. For a long time, I thought making me choose my own instrument of punishment was awful. I later found out that it was really quite godly.

Can you imagine God allowing you to choose your own punishment? In 2 Samuel 24, David had sinned by taking a census when God had told him not to. The act was a signal that David didn't trust God and was checking to see how big his army was. God was not happy and He decided to punish David, but He made a deal with him. God said, "I'll tell you what. I'm going to give you a choice between three punishments. Pick one, and I'll serve it up."

That is the most amazing thing to me. David messed up and God decided to cut a deal with him. It was multiple choice:

(a) Seven years of famine.

(b) Three months on the run from your enemies.

(c) Three days of pestilence in the land.

Then God said, "Let Me know what you want Me to do to you."

I would have said, "There has got to be a choice 'd' in this thing, Lord!" I love David's response. He said, *"I am in a great strait"* (2 Samuel 24:14). The *New Living Translation* says, *"This is a desperate situation!"* No kidding! David continued, *"Let us fall now into the hand of the LORD; for his mercies are great: and let me not fall into the hand of man."* David figured he was safer in God's hand of chastisement than anywhere else. He knew it would be painful. But he chose the merciful hand of God.

You too have a choice. You've already made some decisions that damaged you and marred your relationship with God. He wants to correct that. You can try to control your own life, try to fix your own messes, and leave yourself at the mercy of the world, or you can let the Potter put you back on the wheel and work on you. There have been times in my life when, just like David, I messed up. I've tried to run away from the wheel. There are times when I knew I was under the chastening hand of God, and I have learned to take Him seriously because I know that He is very serious about my sin. I learned to think twice about disobeying Him or thinking that just because I got away with something once, I'm in the clear.

When we come to respect the chastening of God, He can then take us to another level of relationship with Him. When you were a child, you were on your best behavior solely because of your fear of punishment. But God said that to fear Him is just the beginning of wisdom. That means there's another level. We have to get to the point with God where we resist sin because we know it disappoints Him and it closes the door to greater blessings.

Until I had kids of my own, I didn't understand when my parents would say, "This is going to hurt me more than it will hurt you." I used to figure my mother and father must have been really hurting, because they were wearing me out! Then I had children of my own, and I understood...

When my son, Kendan, was young and he would disobey me, I'd spank him, but it hurt me. As he got older, the bond between us became closer, and discipline and chastening took on a new form. One time he got in trouble at school and he came home crying. I hadn't even said anything to him, but he knew the school had called and that I was waiting for him at home. He came in and said, "Daddy, you're going to spank me, aren't you?" I'll never forget that. I was frustrated, and I was hurt. He was crying over what he had done, and I was so grieved over it that I had a tear in my eye. I said, "Kendan, you have broken my heart. I am so disappointed in you. Get out of my sight." I never touched him, didn't put a finger on him. And we were both hurting.

Do you know what our sin does to God? It breaks His heart, this God who has loved us, provided for us, prospered us, and saved us from so much. We choose to step out of His will, violate His laws, misuse and abuse ourselves and others, and all the while expect Him to bless us.

Sin breaks the heart of God, and if you love God, it should break your heart to do that to Him.

The most amazing thing to me about the passage in Jeremiah is not that the pottery was broken or damaged, not that the vessel was cracked and bruised. Not at all. The most amazing thing was that, in spite of the flaws, the Potter continued to hold it in His hand.

> WHEN WE RESPECT THE CHASTENING OF GOD, HE CAN TAKE US TO A NEW LEVEL OF RELATIONSHIP WITH HIM.

That night before Kendan went to bed, he came to me, put his arms around me and hugged me. He said, "Daddy, I'm sorry." No spanking; but pain. No restriction; but sorrow. No punishment; but repentance. Have you ever had to go to God and say, "Father, I'm sorry"? Have you ever reached that painful place of holy contrition and brokenness, where you have to face the God who deserves nothing less than your best and say, "I did something that I know broke Your heart. I'm sorry. I did something with my body, Your temple. I am sorry. I violated Your law. I stole from You. I sinned. I'm sorry"?

The next morning Kendan got up, and, before he went to school, he came to me and said, "Daddy, are you still mad at me?" I said, "Son, it's forgotten. It's over with. I love you." If we confess our sins, He is faithful and just to forgive us our sins and cleanse us from our unrighteousness (1 John 1:9). That's what happens when we get back up on the wheel. That restoration is the work of the Potter.

Have you ever seen a potter work with a piece of clay? He is constantly dousing it with water to keep it moist and pliable while he works with it. Your water is the Word of God, and if you let God soak you with it and work it into you as He fashions you into the vessel He wants you to be, you will glorify Him and live in the destiny He has planned for you.

UNSEEN HANDS: THE THIRD WILL

So far we have learned that the Potter has a will and that the clay also has a will. But there is one will that you might miss if you slide by the passage too quickly. Remember, the Bible said that the clay was *"marred"* in the hand of the Potter. That could mean that the clay was acted on by an *outside force* or it could mean that the clay made some bad choices. And then there is a third option. That word *marred*, when talking about clay, could also mean that it "contains foreign debris." It means there was something in the clay that was not put there by the clay, but it got mixed up with the clay and thereby marred the vessel produced with it.

The tenses of the verbs in the passage suggest that it was not the Potter who put the imperfections and the foreign particles in the clay. In other words, the Potter is not to blame for the flaws. In fact, the voice of the verb could suggest that *something happened* to the clay.

There is the will of the Potter.

There is the will of the clay.

And then there is the will of someone who did not want to see the will of the clay yield to the will of the Potter: A third will exerted itself and put something in the clay to make it resist the will of the Potter. That third will is the enemy of your soul. He wants to put anything and everything and anybody into your life that will mar and scar and deter you while you try to live your life on the wheel of the Potter.

It's hard enough being on the wheel as it is, but to be attacked and have stuff thrown into the mix puts us in an even more difficult situation. Sometimes the bad choices we make are the results of things the enemy puts into our lives before we're even born. He put it into our parents' lives, and they put it into ours. Is that so far-fetched? Remember the parable of Jesus that likened the kingdom of God to a man who planted a field, and while he was sleeping, the enemy came and sowed tares among the wheat. That would be just like the devil. You're trying to be the best little clay you can be, up there on the Potter's wheel, when something rises up and throws you off-kilter. Then, instead of making a smooth turn, you start to get all wobbly in the hand of the Potter. And the next thing you know, He's pounding you down to an unrecognizable lump.

> REMEMBER THAT YOU ARE ON THE WHEEL OF A POTTER WHO KNOWS WHAT HE'S DOING.

But don't lose hope! First of all, remember that you are on the wheel of a Potter who knows what He's doing. He knew the condition of the clay when He picked it up. He knew how much junk, debris, and foreign matter were in it. And when you started wobbling back and forth on the wheel, He was not surprised.

You may ask, then, If the Potter knew the clay was that messed up, why did He decide to do anything with it? That is called *grace*. You are not who you are because you're so wonderful; you are who you are because the Potter knew what to do with you. You see all the mess inside; He sees His plans for you. You see flaws and scars; He sees a bride for His Son, pure and free from all the stuff the enemy put in there. You see what went into making the clay; God sees what's going to come out of His efforts on your behalf.

He put you on that wheel and let you go round and round. As you turn, He has His hands on you, molding you, caressing you, working you. His hands feel the bumps and lumps beneath the surface. His hands work the debris to the surface. He knows when to make you stand taller, and He knows when you need a good pounding down. There is a battle of wills on the wheel. It is the will of the Potter to bring forth a vessel that brings glory and honor to His workmanship. There is the will of the clay that can choose to resist or yield to the will of the Potter. Then there is the will of the enemy, whose goal is to circumvent the work of the Potter by throwing as many impure things into the clay as he can.

Whose will is the strongest? The enemy would have you believe that it's either your will or his that is in control. If he can get you to believe that, then you will live the rest of your life at his mercy. The truth is, the enemy's will is stronger than yours—*unless you surrender your will to the Potter!* Think about it. If the clay continues to resists the hand of the Potter, eventually the Potter will remove it from the wheel, and it will dry up and become useless. But if you give your will to the Potter and stay on the wheel, He will work every scar and flaw out of you.

One of the steps in making pottery involves putting it into the oven to harden it. There's no way around it, child of God. You will see the fire. The enemy would have you believe that the fire can destroy you. However, let me tell you a little secret about making pottery: It's not the fire that makes the pot firm; it's the architectural integrity of the pot *before* it goes into the flames that ensures its stability. If the pot was not made correctly before it was put into the oven, if there are air pockets or debris still in it, then the vessel will collapse or explode under the pressure of the heat. Understanding this will be a valuable weapon for your fight against the wiles of the devil.

When a potter puts a vessel into the fire, he is already sure it can take the heat. The potter never puts a piece of work into an oven until he is certain that it will not be destroyed by the high temperatures it will be exposed to. However, the potter can only be as certain as his own knowledge, skill, wisdom, and ability to control outside factors. Who is your Potter? God knows everything, can do anything, is perfect in wisdom and power, and nothing is beyond His control. And He is the same yesterday, today, and forever, so He can be perfectly certain that if you have to go into the fire, you will be ready to endure the heat.

Some people think God uses the fire to find out if you can stand up in the heat. *He* already knows you can—that's why He put you in it. He wants to show you that you can take it. Whenever you find yourself under pressure, in the heat of life, remember whose hands you were in before you hit the oven. Remember who shaped you and built you. Remember who knows you more intimately than you know yourself.

Don't try to get out of the fire before it's time. That is also under the Potter's control. His knowledge and wisdom are perfect. There are no hands more skilled than His when it comes to shaping destiny. Walking with God is constantly synchronizing our will with His will. It is having the desire to have only the desires that He desires you to desire. If He doesn't want it for me, then I don't want to want it.

Spiritual maturity is learning how to line up our will with the will of the Potter. That means submitting when our will is clearly different from His. That's when we have to practice what I call the theology of "nevertheless." *Nevertheless* is that point where you say, "Nevertheless, not my will, but Yours, Lord." Anytime you ask God to let His will be done, you automatically petition Him to undo your own will. You're done asking if there's a Plan B. You're talked out, cried out, and run out. If there is another way, you don't want to know it. You just want to know which way *He* wants you to go.

> THERE ARE NO HANDS MORE SKILLED THAN GOD'S WHEN IT COMES TO SHAPING DESTINY.

Stay on the wheel, dear Christian. I promise you, it is safer for you to be in the hand of God than any other place. God is the only guarantee you have in this life. Anywhere outside of His will leads to destruction. Marriages are not made in bed; they're made on the wheel. Ministries are not built in schools; they are fashioned on the wheel of the divine Potter. Character, integrity, holiness, faith, long-suffering, wisdom, forgiveness, fearlessness, love are all shaped on the wheel. Everything God desires for your life is on His wheel; and as with all things regarding the hand of God, the only right response is acceptance of that wheel.

IN *His* IMAGE

Charles Swindoll wrote, "Acceptance is taking from God's hand absolutely anything He chooses to give us, looking up into His face in love and trust—even in thanksgiving—and knowing that the confines of the hedge within which He has placed us are good, even perfect, however painful they may be, simply because He Himself has given them."

"Behold, as the clay is in the potter's hand, so are you in My hand. Cannot I do with you as this potter?" says the Lord.

Well?...can He?

Ten

BELOVED PURSUIT: THE HEART OF GOD

> "What does it look like? It has hands to help others,
> feet to hasten to the poor and needy, eyes to see
> misery and want, ears to hear the sighs and sorrows
> of men. That is what love looks like."
> —Augustine

We have arrived near the end of our study of how man physically reflects the image of God. For all of our luxuriating in this examination of the person and personality of the One by whom and in whom we exist, we have arrived where we began: the heart of God. It is, after all, the heart of God that desires to be known and that moves heaven and earth to reveal Himself to us.

When we speak of the heart, various images and terms come to mind—usually emotional ones. We seldom think about the heart in terms of the physical organ that beats in our chests. During a physical checkup perhaps we think of it that way, but for the most part we use "heart" to refer to our sentiments, affections, and passions—how we *feel*.

Scripture employs various ideas using the heart:

The heart is the center of our desire, the seat of our will. To speak of *a heart issue* is to address something that goes to the very core of who we are.

Proverbs 23:7 says a man is *"as he thinketh in his heart."*

Thinking is usually associated with the mind, but the writer of that proverb said that the real *you* thinks with your heart.

Paul stated that it is with the heart that a man believes unto righteousness. He also said that confession is made with the mouth unto salvation (Romans 10:10).

Jesus told the Pharisees that out of the abundance of the heart, the mouth speaks (Romans 10:10 and Matthew 12:34).

The psalmist said, *"The fool hath said in his heart, There is no God"* (Psalm 14:1). This means that the person who believes that there is no God, the person who rejects the existence and personhood of God, is a "fool."

Deuteronomy 6:5 says we are to love the Lord with all our heart—meaning our entire will and being.

In Psalm 19:14 the psalmist prayed, *"Let the words of my mouth and the meditation of my heart"* be acceptable in God's sight because the heart is the center of who we are mentally, morally, and spiritually.

We *consider* in our heart.

We *know* in our heart.

We *remember* in our heart.

A person having a special place in our heart is one who has our devotion to him or her. When we give our heart to someone, it means we love that person.

The heart is the resting place for our joy and our courage.

Pain comes into our heart. Desire, despair, sorrow, and fear all reside in our heart.

In John 14 Jesus told the disciples that they shouldn't be troubled in their hearts at His leaving.

The heart is where our integrity is birthed and nurtured. It is where the real "us" lives.

The Lord tries our hearts, refines our hearts, searches our hearts, and knows our hearts because that is where the true person lives. *Where our treasure is, there will our hearts be also.* There's a connection between our hearts and our treasure.

We understand that God is a Spirit, but He speaks to us in terms we can understand and process cognitively. In this book so far, we have examined the face of God, the ears of God, the eyes, mouth, arms, and hands of God. All those are *anthropomorphic* depictions of Him, meaning "in the form of man." When we look at ourselves, we can see those things on our own human forms. However, when we come to the issue of *the heart of God,* the representation is not so much anthropomorphism as it is *anthropopathism*: God in terms of *human feelings*, as opposed to form.

> GOD IS A GOD OF EMOTIONS, AND THE HEART OF GOD REPRESENTS HOW HE FEELS.

When we look at the heart of God, as with our own heart, we will examine it for its emotional facets. God has an emotional personality. We've looked at some passages that talk about the anger of God and the joy of God. There are several passages in the Psalms that refer to God's laughing. The divine, holy God actually laughs—imagine that. It's interesting what He laughs at. He usually laughs at those people who think they'll get away with things. He laughs at them because He knows their just punishment is coming.

God is a God of emotions, and when we talk about the heart of God, we consider how He *feels*. What's interesting about the fact that He has a heart is not that He has one. What's fascinating is the guy He picks to lift up as the *example* to those of us who seek to understand God's heart. From Genesis to Revelation, only *one* person is referred to by God as *"a man after mine own heart."* That man is found in Acts, where he is identified in Paul's sermon to the people at Antioch as he harkens back to 1 Samuel 13:14:

> *And when he had removed him [Saul], he raised up unto them David to be their king; to whom also he gave testimony, and said, I have found David the son of Jesse, a man after mine own heart, which shall fulfill all my will.*
>
> (Acts 13:22)

Saul was Israel's first king. When God removed him, He raised up David and gave a testimony about him. He said that David was *a man after His own heart*. The people didn't say that about David. David didn't say that about David. *God* said it about David.

God said, "I have found this man David." In reading the context in which David came to be king, we find that there was literally a search; God actually sought out a king for Israel. And out of all the people in Israel, He settled on David as the guy who was the kind of person God was looking for, a man who God said was after His very own heart. That is not said about anybody else in Scripture! The closest we get to it is in Jeremiah 3 where God said, "I will give you pastors after My own heart," but those were unnamed people. Here God went to great length to identify and spotlight David, the shepherd boy. David the king. David the giant-slayer, the great warrior, and the great leader in battle. David, beloved of God. In fact, his name means "beloved." David was God's man, called to lead God's people. David was the king who designed the temple, the very house of God. David was the man acknowledged by the Almighty as "a man after My heart."

If we were to take a poll and ask people what they remember about David, most of them would probably come up with a lot more than, "He was a man after God's heart." Most of us, when we think about David, think about a different David than that.

David the king. Sure, he was a king. He was also an adulterer.

David the warrior. Yes, he was that, but he was also a murderer.

David the great leader. True, but he was also a liar and a cheater.

David was selfish. He was arrogant. He abused his power. He misused his position. He betrayed his friend and had him killed; then he was involved in a conspiracy to cover it up. He was an adulterer. I don't know whether to scratch my head or shout. If this is the criteria God uses to pick His favorites...then there should be a few more guys on His list! I mean, a guy like David is absolutely amazing. The only one in Scripture to whom God gives that very personal endorsement, "A man after My own heart."

One writer said David was an insoluble enigma; an irreconcilable paradox. Holy man of God, yes, but with hellish ways. That will make you wonder, until you realize that if you focus on David, you'll miss the point completely.

The point in the passage is not so much the commentary about David's heart as it is a revelation about *God's* heart. Although David was the only one of whom it was said that he was a man after God's heart, if we make him our model and our focus, we'll stay in a spiritual quandary. The issue is not that David had such a perfect heart, but that he had a heart that was *running after a perfect Heart*. Go after the heart that David was after, and you'll be on the right track. David's goal was to access and acquire the heart of God.

> DAVID HAD A HEART THAT WAS RUNNING AFTER THE PERFECT HEART OF GOD.

Many people make themselves comfortable choosing role models and examples that they know they are better than. Some look at David and figure he's not so hard to beat. We may have done a little cheating in our lives, maybe even told a few lies. But come on—the man was a sneaky, cheating, lying, wife-stealing, murdering, arrogant, fornicating, manipulating, selfish hypocrite. Most of us aren't that bad. And we might put together a pretty good argument before God on that point—*if* David were our model. But the emphasis is on the heart of God that David was after.

The story of David reads like a cable TV miniseries. The situation with Bathsheba alone is enough to warrant a parental warning. We all know the story, as told in 2 Samuel: David saw Bathsheba and decided that he wanted her. So he sent for her, slept with her, and got her pregnant. All the while knowing that she was married to Uriah, a friend and an officer in his army.

Bathsheba was married to Uriah. Now, it might not have been quite as bad if David hadn't known that, but Scripture says he asked about Bathsheba and then he sent for her. He knew who her family was and who her husband was. He slept with her, and she got pregnant. David figured he would cover up his sin; so he sent for Uriah, who was out on the battlefield—which is where David should have been, as king and leader of the armed forces. The Bible says it was the time *"when kings go forth to battle,"* but David *"tarried still at Jerusalem"* (2 Samuel 11:1). Tarrying when you're not supposed to will get you in trouble every time.

When Uriah showed up, David tried to get him to sleep with his wife so he'd think the baby was his. That didn't work because loyal Uriah wouldn't think of sleeping with his wife while his men were still out at war. So, instead of going home to Bathsheba, he slept on the ground outside. That messed up David's Plan A.

Plan B was even more cold-blooded: He sent Uriah back out to war with a note for Joab, his commanding officer, ordering Joab to put Uriah on the front line of the most heated battle, pull his support troops back, and expose him to certain death. David wrote all that in a note, and he had Uriah deliver it! Of course, Uriah had too much integrity to read the note.

Uriah got killed—it was premeditated murder—and David married his widow.

...And that was a man after God's heart?! Something is wrong with that picture! But remember, this is not about David's heart; it's about the *heart that David is after.* God chose

David, who is seemingly the most amazing choice imaginable in all of Scripture because of the negative things we know to be true about the man. We don't remember that he built great cities. We don't remember the design for the temple that God gave him. Like most people, the bad things, the appalling things, are what lodge in our mental archives. But God is not like us. He doesn't look at outward appearances; He looks at the heart. In fact, He said exactly that to the prophet Samuel just before He had him anoint the teenage David to be the future king of Israel. God saw something in David's heart. He saw something in his heart that appealed to Him. What did He see?

When you are studying Scripture and you want to get a deeper understanding or insight of a particular concept or word, there is a useful hermeneutical tool called *the law of first mention*. One way to get a handle on a Bible word or a concept is to find out when it was first mentioned in the Bible. Gaining an understanding as to how it was used the first time, could help with later references. So, if we want to comprehend something about the heart of God, it is helpful to go back and find out when, how, and where Scripture first refers to God's heart.

ABOUT GOD'S HEART

The law of first mention takes us back to Genesis 6. Here is the setting: We are in the days leading up to the Great Flood, preparing for the destruction of the world by water. God is about to open the windows of heaven and pour out rain for forty days and forty nights. Genesis 6 sets the stage for this period in the history of the world, telling why God is about to destroy His creation:

BELOVED PURSUIT: THE HEART OF GOD

And God saw that the wickedness of man was great in the
earth, and that every imagination of the thoughts of his
heart was only evil continually. And it repented the LORD
that he had made man on the earth, and it grieved him at his
heart.   (Genesis 6:5–6)

The *New King James Version* says, "*The* LORD *was sorry that*
He had made man on the earth, and He was grieved." Verse 5 says
something about man's heart. Verse 6 says something about
God's heart. The chronology is significant because the revelation about the heart of God in verse 6 is a response to something that is revealed about the heart of man in the previous
verse.

It says that God saw the wickedness of man's heart. The
word *wicked* has to do with depravity and destructive sinful-
ness. God looked at man, and He looked past all the fluff, the
games, gimmicks, and facades. He looked past public images,
and he checked out man's heart. Like an X-ray, God looked
deep into the center of man, and He saw nothing but wickedness. To be accurate, He saw that the whole mind, heart, and
consciousness of man, as well as all of his purposes and desires, were consumed with wickedness all day, every day. He
saw utter corruption in the heart of man. He saw the antith-
esis of everything that He considered good, which means He
did not see Himself in their hearts.

God knows that in order to get to know a person, you
have to get to know his heart. Many of us make decisions and
commitments based on the fronts that people put up to impress us. We are enamored with surface trappings. Some of
us need so much attention that we don't bother to go beyond
the fluff. As long as somebody is validating or affirming us,

we're okay. Flowers are good, and so are nice dinners. However, there is more to a relationship than flowers and food. You have to make sure that you get into the very core of who a person is before you commit your heart to them. You should know about his or her heart, not how good he kisses, how fine she is, or what kind of car he's driving, how great she cooks. You'd better know *who* that man is under that three-piece suit, and you won't find that out by taking it off of him. You need to know *who* that woman is without that fancy makeup or those academic letters behind her name. You have to know who people are when nobody is looking. It's a *heart* issue.

When God saw the wickedness in the heart of man, the Word says *He repented*. One version says that God *was sorry*. Another says He *changed His mind*.

There is a profound theological issue raised by that verse: If, as some translations imply, God changed His mind, how could He also be the God "who changes not"? He is omniscient, so how could He be sorry about something He created? How could the God in whom there is no wavering or shadow of changing repent? To say that suggests that God made a decision and then reneged on it. It implies that something happened that God did not know was going to happen, and when it did, He had to adjust His original plans. But if God found out something that He previously did not know, He could not be omniscient. How can God, who is omniscient, omnipresent, and omnipotent, and is the same yesterday, today, and tomorrow, change His mind?

First, we have to understand that the Word of God was not written for God. It was written for man; so everything in it is God's attempt to help man understand God. As we study the heart of God, we find even here that it is presented to us in anthropopathic and anthropocentric terms (that is, in concepts and ideas that we can relate to). When Scripture says that *God changed His mind*, it is an expression that helps us comprehend the seeming inconsistency between what He said at one point in time and what He said at another. However, in order to unravel this seeming theological conundrum, we have to understand that something crucial happened between verses 5 and 6 of Genesis 6...

God made a decision to create man and give man dominion over all things. Man rebelled and turned his heart against the things of God. When that happened, God responded with what appears to be an about-face. What we must always realize is that any consideration of the mind of God must include not only His omniscience, but also His

> BECAUSE GOD IS JUST, HE CANNOT IGNORE SIN. HE MUST RESPOND TRUE TO CHARACTER.

foreknowledge. Foreknowledge means that, in addition to knowing everything, God knows everything about what's going to happen regarding everything He already knows. Therefore, when God makes a decision to bless man, He already knows how man will respond to it, and He already knows how He's going to respond to man's response.

When man responds as God knew that he would, then God moves to counter man's response. Because His nature is just, He cannot ignore sin. When He sees it, He must respond in a way that is true to His character. Thus, what appears to be a change of mind is actually God doing what He had planned to do all along. God knows what we're going to do before we do it, and He knows what He's going to do about what we do.

God planned to bless you, but He knew that because of your free will you would make wrong decisions and disobey. He decided long before you were born what He would do to put you back in line so that He could bless you as He planned to all along. He loves you too much to leave you outside of His will. And He will do all He has to do in order to get you back on track—including chastise you.

Chastisement is God's plan of pulling you off the road you're on, perhaps letting you cool your heels in a ditch for a minute, and then putting you back on the correct path of blessing. You have to realize, though, that He's putting you back on a path He knew you'd veer away from in the first place. So He has a blessing waiting for you when you get your bearings... but it's not a new blessing. *It's the same blessing He had before you messed up!*

I once told my son, Kendan, "When I come home, I'm going to take you shopping." Kendan wanted another pair of shoes. Kendan always wants another pair of shoes. But all such promises come with some built-in assumptions, unstated "givens," when parents make commitments. I came home that day to discover that Kendan had not done his homework. No homework, no shopping. That's one of those assumptions. He knows we don't go to the mall until all homework is done. Of course, he tried to cut a deal. "Tell you what, Daddy," he said. "Why don't we go shopping first, and then when I come back, I'll do my homework." Uh-uh. He got me with that one before. No homework, no shopping.

I went upstairs, and about an hour later, Kendan came in with a sheet of paper. It was his homework. He said, "Can we go shopping now?" On the way to the mall, he looked up at me and said, "I'm glad you changed your mind about going shopping, Daddy." When he disobeyed, it delayed his blessing. But I know my son. I wasn't surprised that he hadn't done his homework, and I knew that when he saw I was withholding his blessing, the homework would get done. When I had gone upstairs, I didn't change my clothes or take off my shoes (even though I felt like getting into bed), because I knew I had to be ready to keep my word if he finished his homework in time.

To Kendan it looked like I had changed my mind. In actuality I was just delivering a blessing that was already earmarked for him before he messed up. It had his name on it. I just had to get him back on track first so he could be in a position to receive it.

God writes Scripture for *our* understanding, not His. It's hard for us to wrap our minds around omniscience. We have a tough time with foreknowledge. In the ways of God, what we can relate to is that what seems to be a change is not a change at all, but a manifestation of the continuation of His will, which comes out of eternity and into time.

> CHASTISEMENT IS GOD'S PLAN FOR PULLING YOU OFF THE ROAD YOU'RE ON.

Just as significant as the concept of repentance in this passage is the definition of the word *repent*. It's much deeper than simply "changing one's mind." It's a great picture word that means "to breathe and to take in and let out a deep breath of pain." God saw nothing good in man's heart, and He let out a deep sigh of pain. He looked at His children and saw that every waking moment of their lives was taken up with thoughts and acts of wickedness, and His breath left Him in a painful moan.

Coupled with God's repenting is His grief. Genesis 6:6 says God *"was grieved in His heart."* That's like being stabbed in the heart. Specifically, it means to inflict pain in the heart. To say that God was grieved in His heart reflects the depth of His pain when He looked on the sin of men. It also displays the depth of God's love for us that His heart could be so affected by our actions. Here was man, created by God, blessed by God, raised up above all creation by God, made just a little lower than the angels, and he's devoid of all the goodness that God had put into him. The sight of it pierced the heart of God, and He let out a sigh confirming the pain it caused Him. The Scripture says man's sin was continual, habitual, and to the core. Man had taken everything that God had poured into him and defiled it, deliberately and maliciously. When God created man, He said that he was "good." But He couldn't say that anymore; and when things degrade to that point, God wants us to know He is hurting.

I've seen that pain. I've stood at funerals with mothers who've cried over the caskets of children who had broken their hearts. They had given all they knew to give, and their reward was rebellion. I've seen that pain. It's the pain that happens in you when you give your heart to someone you trust, support, and count on to support you and stand with you, and betrayal is the answer you receive. When they turn on you, it gets so painful that you find yourself wishing that you had never let them into your life.

God was grieved in His heart when He saw sin. There's a clue there about David. The emphasis on the heart of David is not on the *action* of his sin but on his *attitude* about sin. David, being a man after God's own heart, is not to be seen in his disobedience or his rebellion. He is to be seen in how he regarded sin in his life. David did have a sense of what his sin did to the heart of God, because God's sorrow and grief were duplicated in David's own heart.

God chose David and deemed him to be a man after His own heart before David ever sinned with Bathsheba. An omniscient God of foreknowledge chose David, so there was never anything David did that was a newsflash to God. God knew that He had already put something in David's heart that would ultimately overrule the rebellion of his flesh. So when David went to God after his sin, it was with the same pained heart that God Himself had.

David cried, "Have mercy on me, O God, not according to my own goodness, but according to Your loving-kindness, according to the multitude of Your tender mercies. Blot out my sin. Wash me, because I know I've sinned against You, and I know I've broken Your heart. I'm coming to You, Lord, because I need You to clean me up and fix my heart. I want Your forgiveness, Father, but I'm struggling because I also need something deeper than forgiveness. Every time I look at my life, my sin is all I see. I see stuff in my life that reminds me of my waywardness. I tried to do right by Bathsheba. I married her, but every time I look at her, I'm reminded of my crimes. When I look at my children, I remember the son who died because of me. Lord, my sin is ever before me. I've messed up. I've fallen down. I've blown it—big time. But there's something in me that wants to be like You. I want You to be pleased with me, but I'm so far from that

> THE EMPHASIS ON DAVID'S HEART IS NOT ON HIS SIN BUT ON HIS ATTITUDE ABOUT SIN.

right now. I need You to break the shackles of the guilt. I know what I've done to You. I groan with the pain of it. My heart is pierced and torn over my betrayal of You. Father, purge me."

When you walk in sin too long, you begin to feel dirty. Your hands feel dirty, your feet feel dirty, your mouth is dirty, your mind has wicked thoughts. You try to do right, but every little thing that comes into your mind seems to distract you from the things of God. David needed to be cleaned up. He needed a bath. But he needed more than a surface cleaning. He had something going on beneath the skin. He had a heart problem. And David understood that the solution was not to scrub his heart clean; no amount of soap would do the job. The dirt was there from *birth*.

> *Behold, I was shapen in iniquity; and in sin did my mother* > *conceive me.* (Psalm 51:5)

David understood that God wanted truth in the most inward parts of him. And he knew that simply cleaning his heart wouldn't do it. So he asked God to *"create in me a clean heart"* (Psalm 51:10). The word *create* means "to make or bring into existence from nothing." A brand new heart is what David was asking for. He knew he nothing to give God to work with. If God was going to answer this prayer, He would be working from scratch. But David was a man after the heart of a God for whom nothing is impossible.

A clean heart is one that's pure. That's God's heart. A heart that's righteous. God's heart. David wanted a heart that was upright, innocent, perfect, and free from debris. The heart of God.

What does it mean to be a man or woman after the heart of God? It means you respond to sin the way God responds to it: When He sees sin, He moves to remove it. We are men or women after God's heart when we move to remove sin from our life. Moreover, a heart after God's is a commentary on our attitude toward our attitude. How do you feel about how you feel about your sin? Genesis 6 says that every imagination of man's heart is evil. We can't just stop at what we do. We have to take active steps to abort sin before it is conceived in us. Sin is not born in our hands or on our lips. Sins that defile the body are not born on the skin. Our minds can be wicked. Sin is not only about what we do, but also what we *imagine* doing. God sees beneath our behavior. He sees that ugliness we harbor in our hearts and hide from the world. He wants us to move to *remove* it!

> **WHEN YOU WALK IN SIN TOO LONG, YOU BEGIN TO FEEL DIRTY.**

Many of us want to condemn folks for what they do, when the only reason we didn't do the same thing is because nobody asked us. We didn't get the opportunity to do that particular sin, so we think that lets us off the hook with God. God says *think again*. He holds us accountable for what we *wanted* to do, what we imagined and thought about, what we would have done—that wickedness we *rehearsed in our minds!*

> *Know ye not that your body is the temple of the Holy Ghost which is in you, which ye have of God, and ye are not your own?* (1 Corinthians 6:19)

Fantasizing over pornographic material is not recreation; it is *sin*. You think what you do in the privacy of your own home doesn't matter? What about what you do in the privacy of God's home? When you allow those things to occupy your thoughts, you are painting the walls of God's house with sexual depravity, filth, anger, bitterness, unforgiveness, and envy. David said the only remedy is a brand-spanking-new clean heart crafted by God Himself from scratch.

If we focus on David's sin, we miss the blessing of his *character*. Are we more sinless than David? That's like asking a woman if she's "more pregnant" than another. Sinlessness is absolute: You either are or you aren't—and none of us are.

We could learn a lot from David. For instance, he kept very short accounts with God. When he saw sin, he didn't put off confessing it. When he confessed it, he didn't wait to repent. When he repented, he forsook it immediately. You don't see David doing the same thing over and over. And when he had confessed, repented, and forsaken his sin, David was quick to rejoice and praise God. In fact, he praised God throughout the whole process.

There ought to be more Davids in this world.

A HEART UNVEILED

I want more than anything to have a heart like God's. I struggle with that every day of my life because I know that having a heart like God's is not just about what I do or don't do. It goes to what I think, need, and hide in the dark places of my consciousness. If I could just stop thinking about some things and forget others...But like David, my sin is always before me.

I remember a song we used to sing in church that I still pray from time to time:

BELOVED PURSUIT: THE HEART OF GOD

Give me a clean heart,

So I may serve Thee.

Lord, fix my heart,

So that I may be used by Thee.

Though I'm not worthy

Of all these blessings,

Give me a clean heart,

And I'll follow Thee.*

It's an odd song when you first think about it. I want God to give me a clean heart so I can serve Him. I want Him to fix me so He can use me. That makes sense, but then we jump to not being worthy of all the blessings. What blessings? The blessings of serving God and being used by Him. If you're a man or woman after the heart of God, after a while, you'll stop asking for cars and houses, a husband or wife. There's nothing wrong with those things, they just won't be at the top of your prayer list.

The last two lines grip me. *Give me a clean heart, and I'll follow You.* How do you know when God is creating a clean heart in you? You'll follow Him. Not just to church on Sunday, but to eternity. You'll follow Him when it's comfortable, and when it's not. You'll follow Him when your mother and father won't go with you and your friends talk about you for being "too holy." You'll follow Him when it makes sense and when it doesn't—and especially when it doesn't.

You'll follow Him for one reason and one reason alone: You're after His heart, as David said.

---

*Margaret Douroux, "Give Me a Clean Heart."

> *One thing have I desired of the LORD, that will I seek after;*
> *that I may dwell in the house of the LORD all the days of my*
> *life, to behold the beauty of the LORD, and to inquire in his*
> *temple.* (Psalm 27:4)

We see David praying all the time in Scripture. He didn't make a move without consulting God. He praised God in prayer, interceded on behalf of others, repented, and petitioned. And yet here we find him saying he desired only one thing: to dwell inside God, to see His heart, to commune with Him, all the days of his life. That means every prayer, petition, praise, and plea of David was subject to that one desire.

When you're after God's heart, your desires get streamlined. If something doesn't bring you closer to the heart of God, you don't want it. Pretty soon, you lose your taste for some things you thought would never leave you alone. Why? Because your life will become saturated and soaked in your need to see more of God. A heart after God's heart is not one without hopes or dreams. It is simply a heart that wants what God wants. Did you ever consider that you might be able to fulfill the desires of God's heart?

> **WHEN YOU'RE AFTER GOD'S HEART, YOUR DESIRES GET STREAMLINED.**

Lord, what can I do for You today?

A miraculous thing happens when you sincerely seek to know the desires that reside in the heart of God. He tells you exactly what He wants; not in your ear, but in your person. When God reveals His wishes to you, they become a part of you. Remember, you are changed by what God reveals to you. That's why Jesus said that abiding in Him means that whatever you ask for *will be done*. When you really seek the heart of God, His compassion becomes your compassion. His yearnings become yours. You become what He wants. A person after God's heart cannot see the righteous forsaken nor hear the cries of the oppressed and not respond. The heart of God breaks when it sees sin, not because of the offense, but because of the death that comes by it. Likewise, your heart will break when you see souls dying.

What does the heart of God look like?

It looks like His eyes, which see every part of me and love me anyway.

It looks like His mouth, that encourages me and teaches me.

It looks like His ears, which hear me and listen for me.

I can see the heart of God in His hands as they deliver me, mold me, chastise me, and comfort me.

His heart is the shape of His smile. The heart of God is God. And as I behold His image, my image is transformed to reflect the glory of His heart within me. My eyes begin to see like His eyes. My mouth utters His words. My hands delight to do the things He would do.

And what is the greatest desire of God's heart? That your image would run after His!

Lord, what can I do for You today?

"Run after Me. Seek Me. Be curious about Me. Wonder about Me. Examine Me. Study Me. Look for Me. Look at Me. Pursue Me. Want Me. Thirst for Me. Hunger for Me. Desire Me. Reach for Me. Come to Me. Grope for Me. Call out to Me.

Listen for Me. Speak to Me. Turn to Me. Return to Me. Lie down with Me. Wake up with Me. Work with Me. Serve Me. Praise Me. Thank Me. Accept Me. Adore Me. Sup with Me. Drink of Me. Eat of Me. Enjoy Me. Inhale Me. Exhale Me. Live in Me. Die with Me. Love Me. Be loved by Me."

How do you know when you have found the heart of God? It's when you know, as David did, that you are His beloved. When you know, in your own heart, that you are unconditionally, unceasingly, relentlessly, intentionally, and unfailingly loved by the fathomless wonder...named *God*.

ABOUT THE AUTHOR

$\mathcal{D}$r. Kenneth C. Ulmer, one of the most sought after speakers of our time, has been pastor of Faithful Central Bible Church (formerly Faithful Central Missionary Baptist Church) in Inglewood, California, since January of 1982. During his tenure, the congregation has grown from 350 to more than 13,000.

Dr. Ulmer received his bachelor of arts degree in broadcasting/music from the University of Illinois. After accepting his call to the ministry, Dr. Ulmer was ordained at Mount Moriah Missionary Baptist Church in Los Angeles, California, in February 1977. In 1979, he founded Macedonia Bible Baptist Church in San Pedro, California. His thirst for knowledge led him to continue his graduate work at Pepperdine University, Hebrew Union College, and the University of Judaism. In June 1986, he received the doctor of philosophy degree from Grace Graduate School of Theology, Long Beach, California, which became the West Coast Campus of Grace Theological Seminary. In May 1999, he received his doctor of ministry from United Theological Seminary.

In June of 1989, Dr. Ulmer was awarded an honorary doctor of divinity from Southern California School of Ministry. He served as a council member of the California Attorney General's Policy Council on Violence Prevention, and as a member of the board of directors of the Rebuild Los Angeles (RLA) Committee, designed to rebuild Los Angeles after the civil unrest of 1992. In 1994, he participated in the study of Ecumenical Liturgy and Worship at Magdalene College at Oxford University in England, and continues his studies at Christ Church and Wadham College at Oxford.

He has served as an instructor in pastoral ministry and homiletics at Grace Theological Seminary, instructor of African-American Preaching at Fuller Theological Seminary in Pasadena, an adjunct professor at Biola University (where he has served on the Board of Trustees) and Pepperdine University, and he mentors in the doctor of ministry degree program at United Theological Seminary in Dayton, Ohio. Currently he is an adjunct professor at The King's College and Seminary in Los Angeles (where he is a founding board member).

In 1994, he was consecrated Bishop of Christian Education of the Full Gospel Baptist Church Fellowship, where he also sat on the Bishops' Council. Dr. Ulmer has served on the board of directors of the Gospel Music Workshop of America, the Pastor's Advisory Council for the City of Inglewood, and the board of trustees of Southern California School of Ministry.

In early 2000, Dr. Ulmer was installed as the Presiding Bishop over the Macedonia International Bible Fellowship, with churches representing the countries of Zimbabwe, Namibia, Angola, Republic of the Congo, South Africa, and the United States.

Dr. Ulmer is an accomplished writer and published author of three books: *A New Thing* (a reflection on the Full Gospel Baptist Movement), *Spiritually Fit to Run the Race* (a guide to godly living) and *The Anatomy of God* (revised and updated as *In His Image: An Intimate Reflection of God*).

Dr. Ulmer is a devoted husband and father. He and his wife of over twenty-six years, Togetta, two daughters, RoShaun and Keniya, and son, Kendan, are residents of L.A., California.

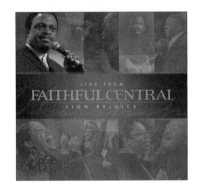

LIVE FROM FAITHFUL CENTRAL
ZION REJOICE

An experience of worship captured live is the only way to describe this phenomenal recording at the renowned Faithful Central Bible Church in Los Angeles, California. Under the covering of Bishop Kenneth Ulmer, the worship leaders, praise team, choir, and an assembled world-class band come together for an explosive evening of worship Faithful Central style. Masterfully produced by award-winning "Choir Maestro" and esteemed industry veteran Joe Pace, this mega church's project will be established as a landmark among all others.

You'll be uplifted by the title track "Zion Rejoice," mesmerized by the magical voice of Daryl Coley singing "In This Place," and ready to transform any car or living room into a tabernacle of praise from the sounds of "Welcome." Inspirationally, Bishop Ulmer shared encouraging insights throughout the record, with the same anointing that has built Faithful Central into a force of over 7,000 strong. Musically, the band renders a thrilling and riveting delivery under the leadership of the renowned Warryn Campbell.

Don't miss this powerful experience of worship—Faithful Central makes *Zion Rejoice!*

CD • UPC: 000-768-337-127

VISIT OUR WEBSITE AT
www.faithfulcentral.com

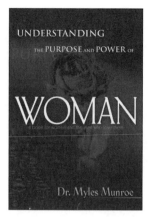

Women of every culture and society are facing the dilemma of identity. To live successfully in today's world, women need a new awareness of who they are and new skills to meet life's challenges. Best-selling author Dr. Myles Munroe helps women to discover their God-given purpose and potential. Whether you are a woman or a man, married or single, this book will help you to understand *the woman as she was meant to be.*

Understanding the Purpose and Power of Woman
Dr. Myles Munroe
ISBN: 0-88368-671-6 • Trade • 208 pages

Understanding the Purpose and Power of Men
Dr. Myles Munroe
ISBN: 0-88368-725-9 • Trade • 224 pages

The male is in crisis. Today, the world is sending out conflicting signals about what it means to be a man. Many men are questioning who they are and what roles they fulfill in life—as males, as husbands, and as fathers. Best-selling author Dr. Myles Munroe examines cultural attitudes toward men and discusses the purpose God has given them. Discover the destiny and potential of *the man as he was meant to be.*

WHITAKER HOUSE

proclaiming the power of the Gospel through the written word
visit our website at www.whitakerhouse.com